HOW TO MAKE _____ _ ___ ADVERTISING CREATIVE
SIMON VEKS____

D0536191

Laurence King Publishing

Contents

Foreword
DAVID DROGA

This book is about the qualities you need to be successful in advertising, beyond being good at actually doing the job. Now, I don't necessarily agree with every single word in here—there are so many different opinions in our industry, it would be amazing if any two individuals did agree on absolutely everything.

But what I wholeheartedly agree with is the principle that your success will be determined by a lot more than just how good you are.

For me, it's your attitude that's the key.

For a start, being hard-working should be a given. Always. If you're new in an agency, you need to work hard so you stand out from the people who are already there, and so you can create your own opportunities. At the other end of the spectrum, if you're a CD or an ECD, you need to work hard because you can't ask people to work hard for you if you're not prepared to work hard yourself. I don't expect my people to work all weekend, but I do want them to work hard. The formative years are especially important—they determine your trajectory.

Above and beyond that, I believe the attitude that creatives most need is one of openness…a willingness to learn from people who have experience, people who've already made lots of mistakes.

Then there's finding your voice. A lot of creatives start out trying to emulate the style of a David Abbott, or whoever. You need to have the confidence to answer a brief in the way you think is right.

Some of you reading this may be studying advertising at college. I'm a huge believer in education—in fact I'm on the board of VCU Adcenter—but the one caveat I have for ad students is to bear in mind that you are spending a lot of your time studying old work, which inevitably means you can end up trying to replicate stuff from the past, instead of looking to the future. Students need to understand how what we do has changed. We're still storytellers, but it's not about a story that starts and finishes within the 30 seconds of a TV ad any more. Our job now is more about instigating a story, and letting it go. We can create momentum. Our work doesn't have to be as disposable as before.

When the time comes for the student to get their first job, attitude is crucial. When I'm looking at a young team, I'm not just looking at their work. I'm looking for talent, of course, but also enthusiasm, and restlessness. I look for people who are fascinated by the broader world, not just the world of advertising. I look for people I can teach, but who can also educate me.

And once you're in a job, the right attitude never ceases to be important. Being in a long-established team is advantageous in that you can develop short-cuts, and a great understanding with each other, but you can also get into bad habits. When I see solutions come back from a team that over time are overly consistent —always the same tone, the same emotion—then I can tell it's coming more from them, and not from the brief or the product, and that's not good. I like to mix teams up, put different types of people together—designers, digital guys. Whatever it takes, you constantly need to be challenging yourself.

I would recommend every creative to consider making a country move at some point. I've ended up making several, and I learned so much in each country. Australia taught me that advertising can be fun. Asia taught me you can create ripples from wherever you are. London taught me craft. The Publicis global job taught me about the business side of advertising. Then there's what you learn about the different cultures… different music….

When you eventually get to be an ECD or have your own agency, you realize that success doesn't just come from people's talent but by putting them in the right environment. You need to create the right environment for great work to happen. Beanbags and bright paint are not going to make the work better—it's not about props. But people have got to feel comfortable, and a building with plenty of space and light can help achieve that.

Be ready to have your principles tested. It's great to have principles, but not so easy to stand by them when you have people's salaries to pay. Will you work with any client, to pay the bills? Or will you turn work down? You'll need to know the answer to that question.

I hope you glean from this book some of the behaviors that lead to success. Because even when you have your own agency, your success will stem largely from your attitude, just as it did when you were a student.

Introduction

HOW TO MAKE IT AS AN ADVERTISING CREATIVE

This book is aimed at anyone who is considering becoming an advertising creative, is studying to become one, or already is an advertising creative but would like to become a better one.

The difference between this and other advertising books is that this book will not teach you how to have ideas or write advertisements.

There are books already in existence that deal with the craft side of things; it is also taught extensively in colleges. What is never taught, however, is the collection of skills that you need to make it as an advertising creative above and beyond the ability to write good adverts.

This book will teach you how to get the best out of the people you work with, such as account planners, photographers and directors. It will teach you how to be successful at getting creative directors to buy into your ideas and how to present your work to clients. There's lighter stuff too, like a discussion on whether what you wear is important, and how to argue with your partner.

Getting a job as an advertising creative is not easy. When I started at Watford College, our tutor told us solemnly that not all of us would get jobs. We thought he was trying to knock our confidence, before building it back up again, like at Marine Camp. Actually, he was telling the truth. Only two-thirds of us ended up getting jobs in advertising.

Not only is it difficult to get a job, it's also hard to keep your job in this highly competitive industry. Five years out of college, only half of us still had jobs. After 15 years, we're down to a handful. However, those of us who are still in advertising are now creative directors, some even contemplating their own agency start-ups.

And that's why I believe this book is necessary. I'm convinced that those of us who went on to succeed in advertising aren't necessarily the ones who were the most talented, but the ones who combine some talent with what you might call "savvy." This book aims to teach you that savvy.

This book will teach you the intangible skills that are essential if you are to get a job, survive, thrive and ultimately make it big in one of the most exciting industries on the planet.

P.S. After reading this book, you might assume all creatives are male. That's incorrect. Although I've written "he" throughout, this is purely to avoid the cumbersome "he or she" phrase.

GETTING
A JOB

CHAPTER 1
DO YOU HAVE WHAT IT TAKES TO BE A CREATIVE?

Some say the best creatives are sponges—obsessively soaking up whatever's going on in the world. Then again, it's also said that the best creatives have tunnel vision—they're mollusk-like creatures with obstinately thick shells who ignore outside influences, determined to define their own territory.

WHAT KIND OF PERSON MAKES A GOOD CREATIVE?

Some see a creative as an extrovert, fizzing with a profusion of ideas, sparking off the energy of his colleagues. Alternatively he's a loner, who will retreat into the woods—or Starbucks—and spend hours or days without human contact, until a single monolithic creative idea looms out of his subconscious.

So no one really knows, and the reason no one knows is that there isn't such a thing as a creative type. The most obvious divide is that between typically word-loving copywriters and visually biased art directors (most advertising is produced by creative teams, consisting of one copywriter and one art director—more on this later).

> But in general, in an advertising agency creative department you will find the most diverse group of people imaginable. That's half the appeal.

There is, of course, a *stereotype* of the advertising creative. Watch any movie about advertising and you'll see that we're all crazy. In *How to Get Ahead in Advertising*, Richard E. Grant suffers a psychotic breakdown so serious he believes he has grown a second head; in *Crazy People* (the clue is in the title) Dudley Moore spends the majority of the film as an inmate in a mental hospital, and molds his fellow psychiatric patients into a creative department.

In reality, many of us look perfectly normal. No nation, race, sex, or religion has a monopoly on creative ability. Nor does any particular personality type dominate.

This was brought home to me when my agency sent eight young creative directors on a training course, part of which involved taking the Myers-Briggs personality test.

All eight of us scored completely differently.

Some were introverted, some extroverted. Some were "thinking" types, some "feeling" types.... Some were spontaneous people, others more considered.

The only area we all had in common was a strong bias toward making decisions based on our intuition, rather than seeking to assemble the evidence.

INTUITION

The psychologist in charge of the program confirmed that in over 20 years of testing creative professionals, she was yet to come across *one* without this strongly developed sense of intuition.

The best creative director I have ever worked under had truly outstanding instincts. My art director and I used to liken him to a dog, with an incredible ability simply to "smell" a good idea. He never read research reports, but he always knew what consumers thought. He never enquired into how a product was made or what it contained, but he had an instinctive understanding of what its appeal would be. He never spent more than 1.5 seconds looking at a concept we showed him, and never *ever* changed his mind once he decided he liked something, or didn't like it. And, incredibly, 99 percent of the time, he was right. Few of us have such an extreme bias toward intuition.

But it is fair to say that if you're a person who never has hunches, never trusts your instincts, and never judges a situation until you have all the proper facts… you won't make it as a creative.

DESIRE

Other than intuition, the most important factor in determining whether you will make it as a creative is simply how much you want it.

It is not easy to get a job in advertising—aspiring creatives can spend anything from two months to two years doing "placements," before securing a permanent job. Quite a few give up.

And once you've got a job, it isn't easy to keep it. Your work is highly visible; it could hardly be more so—it's up on giant billboards in the street or played every night on TV. So if you're no good, there's nowhere to hide. You'll get found out.

Plus, it's a competitive field. More people want the jobs than there are jobs available. And plenty of people are prepared to work incredibly hard to get these jobs, and keep them. Advertising is full of passionate and committed people. If you don't have the same desire they do, you won't do as well as them.

As with all competitive fields, those that do well are those with drive and persistence, *as well as* talent.

A STRONG INTEREST IN ADVERTISING

As a child, I used to sing advertising jingles in the playground. My dad sold advertising space for *The Sunday Times*, which in the 1980s was running a fantastic poster campaign through Leo Burnett, and I used to beg him to bring the posters home for me. I put them up on the wall.

It's unlikely that your story is as sad as mine. Nevertheless, a strong interest in advertising is another key predictor of success.

I remember when I was first trying to find a creative partner, I discussed teaming up with a guy who said he wanted to be an art director, but he was also in a band, which rehearsed several times a week.

He never made it as an art director. I don't know if the band was successful either. I suppose focus is helpful for any line of work.

HUSTLE

Initiative is not essential, but over the years I've found it's a quality that many good creatives possess. When I first came into advertising, I thought that juicy briefs would be passed around my workplace on a silver tray, like grapes at a Roman orgy.

That doesn't happen. A lot of this book is about how to make things happen. It's a bit like pinball. If you only flip the flippers, you will never get the high score. You have to learn how to nudge the machine as well. I'm not talking about lying or cheating here. You don't want to "tilt" the machine. But a bit of nudging is to be encouraged.

Especially in the early stages of your career, you should be making things happen for yourself: rooting out good briefs; shooting little bits of film yourself; and making friends in unusual places. All that kind of stuff will help you, and we'll be talking a lot more about it.

THICK SKIN

Before I worked in advertising, I was a journalist. Newspapers have a lot of pages to fill, and I found that 95 percent of what I wrote ended up in the paper.

But in our business, it's the opposite — 99 percent or even 99.5 percent of what you write ends up in the bin.

If there's one thing that characterizes a creative's daily experience, it's rejection.

You are allowed to go into a short period of mourning when an idea that you really love gets killed. But the most successful creatives learn to recover quickly from these setbacks, and "get straight back on the horse."

Even when an idea does get approved, you still need to show toughness—to stand up to the people who start trying to ruin it.

· The account handler may ask you to change your script so the client will like it more.
· The planner may ask you to change it so consumers will like it more.
· The creative director wants awards juries to like it more.
· And the client asks you to change your script so it has a longer product sequence at the end. And in the middle. And the beginning. Actually, can we just have the product all the way through? Make it big. Put a spotlight on it. Some highlights. In fact, why don't we just make it dance? *What do you mean yogurts can't dance?*

DIFFERENT

In all probability, there's something strange about you.

Something weird.

It might be something that everyone who knows you makes comments about, and jokes about, or it might be something only you know about.

It might be your sense of humor, your hobbies, or even just your hair.

But there's definitely something different about you.

It's one of the reasons you are attracted to a creative job, rather than a boring one.

Be proud.

The more different you are, the better. Because to create work that is different and unusual, our industry needs *people* who are different—dreamers, weirdos, obsessives, folks who are "wrongly wired."

If that sounds a bit like you, then you've come to the right place.

CHAPTER 2
HOW TO GET A JOB

GOING TO COLLEGE

If you have picked up this book because you think you might want to work as an advertising creative and you are wondering whether you have to take a college course to get such a job, there is a simple answer to your question.

You do.

The days of getting a copywriter's job off the back of an English degree or an art directing gig straight from art school are long, long gone.

The good news is that the vast majority of colleges are extremely clued up about helping you get a job. They nearly all have good links with the advertising industry and regularly get working creatives to critique students' work (these industry contacts will become crucial after you leave college and begin looking for a job). The tutors will teach you the principles of strategy, ideas, and craft. They will help you build a portfolio that you can take round to agencies.

I didn't do much research before choosing a college, but then again, we didn't have the internet in those days. You do. You must carefully research what colleges are out there. If you know anyone in the industry, or a friend of a friend works in the industry, then speak to them and get a recommendation.

As with anything in life, some colleges are better than others. Don't just rely on their websites and the stuff they send you—these are essentially marketing tools, and without fail they will tell you that their college is brilliant. Find out as much as you can about their reputations from external sources.

How much the college charges in fees and where it is located will both be important factors. Another biggie is how many years the course lasts (some courses are one year, some two, some three). If you already have a degree, you may prefer a one-year course. If you're still in your late teens or early twenties, you may not want to enter the world of work just yet, so a three-year course may be more appropriate for you.

ART DIRECTOR OR COPYWRITER

At some point, you will have to decide whether you want to be an art director or a copywriter. The vast majority of ads are created by a team of two—one art director and one copywriter. (This is another great advantage of college: most creatives meet their partners there.)

On my first day at college, the tutor made one simple request of us. *"Everyone who can draw, stand to my left. If you can't draw, stand on my right."*

We divided ourselves into two more or less equal groups, and he announced: *"Right. All of you on this side of the room, you are the art directors. The rest of you are copywriters."*

That was it. He went on to say that it was just a trial, and anyone who wanted to change could do so at a later date. But no one did.

It's an unconventional method that almost certainly isn't followed at most colleges, but it demonstrates that this is not a decision to agonize over.

Most people find it relatively easy to decide which they are. For example, if you have a strong visual sense, and are interested in things like fashion, cinematography, photography, design, or illustration, then you are an art director.

If you are interested in any kind of writing or screen-writing, then you are probably a copywriter. People who are good at talking—the people whose parents thought they might become lawyers one day—are normally copy-writers too. (Art directors are often strong, silent types.)

The art director/copywriter combination has been the way creative teams have been structured for over 40 years. Very recently, there has been a trend toward teams where neither partner defines themselves explicitly as the copywriter or the art director. That's OK too. For most of the time, you both do exactly the same job—and that is thinking.

All that matters is that, between the two of you, you will be able to cover the various craft skills required; for example, writing copy, choosing photographers, or working with typefaces.

For more information on what copywriters and art directors do separately, see Chapter 9 of this book—*"The differing career paths of art directors and copywriters"*.

*Three very different "landing pages"
of three very different online portfolios.
A digital portfolio shouldn't just showcase
your work, but also your personality.*

WHAT YOU DO AT COLLEGE

You will spend the majority of your time at college actually writing adverts—putting together dummy advertising campaigns for real products. You'll practice working in a variety of media, and with a variety of different partners.

You will also be trained in some of the craft areas, such as typography, copywriting, photography, and art direction, and may be exposed to some general business skills, such as how to pitch and how to give presentations. Depending on the length of your course, you may study advertising in its wider cultural context; analyzing its impact and its history.

I've noticed that how people approach their time at college depends a lot on their age. The students who are taking their first college course, perhaps living away from home for the first time, tend to behave more like typical students—going out a lot, having fun, and crashing their cars (if they have them). Whereas the students who already have a college degree, or are a little older, tend to be more focused on what they can get out of the course, and on getting a job.

Either approach is fine. You have to do what is right for you, and your life-stage.

The relationships you form with your fellow students are crucial. These guys and girls are your peer group, and you will probably stay in touch with them for years to come. They will shape your views on advertising as much as the tutors do. And they are the people who, in future years, you will turn to for advice and, inevitably, compare your career progression with.

There's no secret to getting the most out of your time at college—work hard, have fun, and learn lots. The goal is to leave college with a good partner and a good book.

Your book may not be good enough to get you hired immediately on graduation, but it should be good enough to get you some interesting conversations with working creatives. And they will help you the rest of the way.

PUTTING YOUR BOOK TOGETHER

WHAT FORMAT?

To get a job in advertising, you create dummy or "spec" ads for real clients, put them in a portfolio to showcase your creative talent, then get your portfolio or "book" seen by creative directors. That's the method creatives have been using to get a job for well over 40 years now.

However, the "rules" for what should be in your book are evolving rapidly.

The answer used to be easy: eight ad campaigns (each consisting of three print ads), plus maybe an ambient execution (ambient means non-traditional media, such as ads on the sides of coffee cups, the undersides of airplanes, or stamped onto students' foreheads) and the odd TV storyboard (N.B. without dialogue).

Such was the way it was, for years. But if your book still looks like that, you're doing it wrong. Why? Because creative directors have gone digital-crazy.

Despite growing up in the age of VCRs and vinyl, most creative directors are surprisingly well informed about digital. They're closer to the "business" side of the business—they know that the agency's clients now want great work in non-traditional media, as well as the traditional ones like TV and print.

And as well as retraining their existing creatives, they're looking to the new generation to give them that work. You must be that new generation. Your book must show compelling examples of how brands can exploit the digital space.

Having said all this, you've got to show you can do the traditional media as well, so your book still needs to have lots of great print work. And now that camcorders are cheap, and editing software is free, it's not hard to put together your own TV ads too. If what you produce doesn't look broadcast-standard, it doesn't matter. It shows energy—and this is often the difference between good teams and OK ones.

But more and more you need to demonstrate how to reach consumers in new ways. That means new media, events, ideas for mobile games, TV shows, crazy sh*t... maybe even new products.

And, above all, digital.

The most recent student team whose book my partner and I recommended to the executive creative director at BBH looked like this: nine campaigns, comprising a total of 21 print ads, two TV ads, six digital executions and 31 (!) executions that were ambient/new products/crazy sh*t. Maybe there were a few too many of the latter, but you get the idea.

Fashions in student books change. Make sure you're up-to-the-minute.

Maybe your book shouldn't even be a book, but a website or a CD.

(Actually, I always advise young creatives *not* to put their work onto CD. At least half the time a creative director tries to look at a CD, there is some kind of compatibility problem, and the thing doesn't work. Don't take the risk.)

At the time of writing, the industry is transitioning between the traditional black portfolio with clear plastic sleeves—what you could call an "analog" book—and digital portfolios. It seems likely that all portfolios will be digital within a short space of time.

A digital portfolio is easy to put together—a simple web search will throw up many sites that offer to help you create one, either for free, or for only a small fee. Have a look at a few that other people have done before you do your own. Decide what you think they're doing well and not so well...then copy the elements that you think are good and improve on the bits that aren't. A simple layout and easy navigation are vital.

But whether your work is on a website or on ancient papyrus, the fundamental principles remain the same.

SPENDING YOUR TIME SMARTLY

Naturally, you want it to look presentable—a sloppy portfolio that looks as if it were put together by a right-handed eight-year-old using only his left hand is not what you want. So it's definitely worth spending time crafting your book. But whether your visuals are created on a computer, sketched up with marker pens, or hand-painted with blood from your own veins doesn't make much difference as long as it communicates clearly and looks as if you know what you're doing.

On the other hand, you don't want to spend an *excessive* amount of time crafting the appearance of your work. What your work looks like is far from the most important factor. Creative directors are primarily looking for people who can think, not use a Mac. A lot of people can use a Mac, but not many people can think up brilliant ad campaigns.

Be smart in how you allocate your time. Someone who spends seven hours working on a campaign idea and can then make it look presentable with 20 minutes of Mac time is going to get hired a lot quicker than the person who spends only 20 minutes thinking of ideas and then spends seven hours perfecting the layouts in Photoshop.

Devote the vast majority of your time to thinking. There's a rather large irony in putting a spec book together—the number-one thing creative directors say they're looking for in a student book is "good strategies"—smart thinking about how to sell a product, rather than clever ads per se. And yet, as soon as you get into an agency, the strategies aren't your responsibility, but the responsibility of the planner. Nevertheless, that's what creative directors are looking for. So don't even start to write ads until you have a great strategy to write to.

PICKING YOUR PRODUCT

A lot of teams looking for a job have funny ads in their book. But not many will have ads that, while equally funny (or moving, or whatever), are actually based on an insightful strategy that could really shift a product. Even fewer will have married that thinking to exactly the right brand or product.

Picking the right products to work on is quite an art. The point of your book is to make you look good. Therefore, don't pick products that are "too easy." By this I mean products like a washing machine that runs on only one cup of water—the product itself is so brilliant that it doesn't leave much room for your brilliance. Similarly, avoid products like condoms or AIDS charities—these areas have such a rich potential for powerful advertising that you're giving yourself an unfair advantage. No one is impressed by the darts player who stands 12 inches from the board.

Then again, don't try to hit the bull's-eye from the other end of the room. When I was working on my student book, my partner and I spent weeks and weeks trying to come up with a campaign for a bank—any bank. We never cracked it. Banks are really hard to advertise. They are probably the least visually interesting places on Earth, for a start. All financial services advertising is hard. If you pick a product that is too hard, it's difficult to shine.

I would also advise against choosing unknown products. If you are launching a new product, it takes time to communicate what it is and what it does, before you can get around to explaining why it's good. That makes it hard to create work that communicates quickly. And a slow ad is a bad ad. Creative directors like books that are quick to go through, because they know that in the real world, consumers are pressed for time, and are minimally interested in advertising. Creative directors themselves are pressed for time, and have a lot on their minds. Don't give them campaigns that are hard to work out.

Strip out anything that takes time to read. Don't include a summary of what the brief was, for example, or body copy on print ads. Keep headlines short and avoid TV scripts that require dialogue.

Also, avoid writing campaigns for companies that already have great advertising. Don't write ads for Nike, Volkswagen, or Sony. People can't help but compare—it's human nature. And the comparison won't be in your favor. Better to present good advertising for a product that has never had any. That way, the comparison works for you.

For now, avoid working on the sexy showpiece accounts. There'll be plenty of time for that when you get into an agency.

WHAT SHOULD BE IN YOUR BOOK?

· Print ads
· TV storyboards
· Ambient ads
· Non-traditional/digital ads
· Crazy sh*t!

HOW TO APPROACH AGENCIES

CALLING CREATIVES

Some agencies have specialist in-house recruiters—they will have a title such as creative manager or director of creative services, and you can track them down via the agency's website. But most agencies don't have such people. That means you will have to get hold of the creatives, and calling creatives is hard, because usually they don't pick up the phone.

They may be out on a shoot, or may be working and don't want to be disturbed, or they may be screening their calls. Many ad agency phones have caller ID so it's easy for creatives to ignore numbers they don't recognize. Although it may seem shockingly arrogant that creatives don't even deign to lift their receivers, some creatives get hundreds of calls a month from photographers' agents and directors' representatives, so it's understandable.

You may find your call goes through to voicemail. Don't bother leaving a message—nearly no one calls back. When I was looking for a job, I used to think it was the height of rudeness that creatives never returned my calls. But then I realized…why expect someone to do you the favor of calling you back, just so you can ask them for another favor?

So, if you want to speak to a creative on the phone, you will have to keep calling and calling, and hope that one time they pick up by mistake. But be warned, even when you do get through, it may be awkward. Many creative people are introverts. They don't give good phone.

So my advice is to forget calling.

PERSONALIZE YOUR COMMUNICATIONS

Simply send an e-mail to the team you would like to see, explaining who you are.

Or send a letter. There seems to be a perception out there that "no one reads letters any more." I can assure you that they do. Letters also have an advantage over e-mails in that a letter can't be instantly deleted.

Be aware that most creatives get more requests for help than they have time to see people. You need to get them to choose you, rather than the three or four other teams whose requests are cluttering up their in-box.

The worst thing you can do is send something that looks like a standard e-mail, which you've sent to 40 other teams. If you haven't taken the time to find out about the person you're writing to, then why should they take the time to find out about you?

So when you are writing to a creative, whether by letter or e-mail, you must personalize your communication.

Find out about a piece of work they've done, and mention it in your note. For example, if writing to Juan Cabral, you could start with *"loved your Tate Gallery campaign—it actually inspired me to go there."*

Use personal recommendations too. For example, *"we just saw your old mates Nick & Simon at BBH—they said to say Hi, they liked our book and thought you guys would be good people to help us move it on."*

DO

· Strip out anything too long to read
· Keep headlines short
· Choose a familiar product or service

DON'T

· Create ads for companies that already have great ads
· Choose a difficult company that's almost impossible to do good ads for
· Pick products that are "too easy"

Once the junior teams like your book, see the more senior teams. And when these teams like your book, ask them who is in charge of placements/freelance/hiring (but not before that stage—you'll sound pushy).

You'll rarely (if ever) get an appointment to see a creative director. But that's OK. You don't need to. All you need is a senior team who are on your side, and they will pass your book on to the CD.

And remember, if you are using a traditional or "analog" book, make sure you have multiple copies of it. That way, if one gets "stuck" in some CD's office you still have another to take around.

It's also important to "tailor" your book. If a team doesn't like one of your campaigns, then remove it the next time you go to see them. If an agency is known to be keen on seeing digital work, or ambient, or whatever, then weight your portfolio in that direction.

When you come into an agency for a crit, be friendly, interesting, attentive, clean, and punctual.

And, finally, smile.

I know it sounds corny, but the fact is they're not just looking at a book, they're looking at two people.

It's probably no coincidence that a long time ago, in a galaxy far, far away, the first people to give me and my partner a placement (thank you, Richard and Markham) were two guys that we happened to get along with.

TOP FIVE WORST THINGS THAT COULD ACTUALLY HAPPEN IN A BOOK CRIT, SO YOU SHOULD BE PSYCHOLOGICALLY PREPARED TO EXPERIENCE THEM

1   The creative looking at your book is bored or drunk.
2   They spend longer talking about themselves than they do about your work.
3   They suggest you come back with a completely new book (don't bother—this is a sure sign that they don't like your work and never will).
4   They tell you that your work is rubbish... without telling you why.
5   They don't turn up.

HEADHUNTERS

Some young creatives are scared of headhunters. You shouldn't be. Despite the scary name, they are nothing to be frightened of.

"Headhunters" is an industry term for recruitment consultants. They are often ex-agency employees themselves, and for some reason are nearly always female.

Their job is to see creative directors and find out what kind of teams the agency is looking to hire (what level of experience, salary expectations, and any specific experience needed) and then find creatives to meet that brief.

You can make an appointment simply by calling them, or e-mailing. They will invite you to come to their office, where they will look through your book, and maybe note down some of the campaigns you have in it. At the same time, they are assessing what kind of person you are, and which creative directors they think you'll get on with, either now or in the future. After that, probably nothing will happen.

For that reason, junior creatives sometimes say there's no point contacting the headhunters, not until you have several years' experience. They argue that most first-job creatives get hired from placements, which are arranged by agencies, not headhunters.

There is some truth in that. Most agencies use their senior teams as a filtering system to bring in placement teams. But some creative directors like to ask headhunters if they know of any interesting juniors. Some creative directors even call in 20 or 30 books from headhunters and offer a job—or at least a job trial—to the one they like the best.

I think it's never too early to see a headhunter. But don't just see one of them; see all the headhunters in your market. Some organize schemes like portfolio nights, and it's definitely worth finding out about those. Headhunters are also a good source of industry gossip. They will tell you stories about certain creative directors that may put you off advertising for ever...or make you even keener to get in.

Headhunters. Despite the name, they won't kill you.

HOW TO TURN A PLACEMENT INTO A JOB

MAKING THE SYSTEM WORK

As your book improves, you will start to be offered placements. A placement is sometimes poorly paid, sometimes unpaid, and sometimes expenses-only.

To many creatives, this seems unfair. It is. The placement system favors those who already have some money from somewhere—enough to see them through until they can get a real job at least—or those who are able to live at home, have some other source of income, or have learned to survive by eating everyday household objects instead of food.

However, the supporters of the system say that placement teams are gaining valuable experience, and that by handing out multiple placements, the agencies are giving multiple teams a chance.

This isn't the place to debate the rights and wrongs of the system. The most important thing is to make the system work for you.

Every placement is different. Some agencies run them fairly and well—they take on placement teams for a decent length of time, with a real chance of a job at the end, and give them decent briefs while they're there. Other agencies, sadly, use placement teams as little more than cheap labor.

Nevertheless, the fact remains that while a placement is not the only way to get your first job—you should also be looking for opportunities via friends, contacts, headhunters, and portfolio nights—it's probably the most common way.

The "placement treadmill" can seem daunting: you are regularly starting afresh in an entirely new environment, with totally different people, clients, and systems. But if you work hard while you are on the placement, and you do well, and the agency has a vacancy for a junior team, then there's every chance you could get hired.

HOW TO SHINE

While on placement, you'll most likely be given smaller briefs such as trade ads (ads to go in less glamorous "trade" publications like *Tractor Weekly*), or money-off/special-offer ads to work on. Consider this your opportunity to make yourself useful. Crack them quickly and efficiently, without making a fuss, and without taking up too much of your creative director's time. He will appreciate that. Another reason to get good at the "bread-and-butter" stuff is that while you have work going through the system—being presented to clients, heading into production—then the agency will normally keep you on.

However, you've got to give yourself an opportunity to shine too.

Useful on its own isn't enough. Useful and good is what's wanted.

At most agencies, they will let you have a swing at briefs other than the ones you've been assigned to. Choosing which ones is the tricky part.

Don't waste your time trying to crack the agency's *big kahuna* TV brief. Your chances of success are too slim. You'll be up against the agency's best teams, teams that (for now) can beat you on nine briefs out of ten. Plus they have an unfair advantage—they will know the situation and the client better than you. Also, these kinds of projects take months. Even if an idea of yours does get bought, you will be long gone by then, so won't reap the benefits.

The briefs to go for are the ones in the middle. The promising print briefs for the agency's better clients. Or a TV brief for a smaller client. Projects that don't take too long, and where there isn't too much competition.

Do the things the existing creatives do less of: non-traditional, ambient, stunts, that kind of thing. Make the creative director think that you offer something new to his department. That's better than just being a cheaper and more inexperienced version of what he already has.

USING YOUR PLACEMENT TIME WELL

Fit in. Go to the agency's bar if they have one; make friends with the other young people about the place. If you fit in well, you're more likely to get hired. That's true in any organization. And if you don't fit in well, you're probably in the wrong place anyway.

However, just because you have a placement doesn't mean you stop working on your book. Even if you're really busy. In every moment of spare time, you should be working on your book. If your current placement doesn't lead to a job, you'll need that book to get another one. And the better your book, the quicker you'll find another placement, and the better the agency it will get you into.

Sometimes, after they have done a few placements, junior teams start getting interviews with creative directors, and can get hired on the strength of their book alone. So it's absolutely vital that your book keeps moving forward.

It may be that some of the briefs you are given while on placement lead to work that can go in your book. That's great. You might get some work bought by clients too, and get experience of actually making ads. That's a bonus.

Don't worry if you have been on a placement at the same agency for a while and haven't been hired yet. Some people get hired after being on placement for up to a year. You need to constantly be making calculations. Are there people you are learning from? Is it not too madly busy, so you have some time to work on your book? Is there at least some chance of getting hired?

Don't be afraid to ask questions. Speak regularly to whoever is in charge of the placement system and ask them how you're doing. Ask them if they think there is a chance of a job for you at the agency or not. It's amazing how many creatives complain that they "don't know what's going on." Ask.

Even if they explicitly tell you there is no job for you at this agency, it may be worth staying if you're gaining good experience.

Some people get hired on their first placement. On the other hand, some people do five, ten, or even more before they're offered their first job. Don't worry too much about this. A lot of it is down to luck—you have to do well, which is partly luck, and the agency you are at has to be hiring, which is completely luck. The state of the economy plays a huge role too—in times of recession, you'll be looking for your first job for a lot longer than in times of plenty.

PLACEMENT TIPS

1 Make yourself useful
2 Work on ambient and non-traditional ads
3 Make an effort to fit in
4 Keep adding to your book
5 Ask questions

Ed Morris, former executive creative director of Lowe London, used to give a sheet of paper to all the creatives starting a placement at his agency. This is what it said:

Show me an idea at least every 12 hours (1 working day) without fail.

Make your presence felt. Out of sight out of mind. Out of mind, no job.

F*** the system. No one in the agency should come between you and your future. Walk straight in. It doesn't matter how good you are if I don't get to find out how good you are.

Focus on the work. Don't try and be my friend.

Work on briefs that you haven't been given. Run your own show, don't wait for someone to walk in and "take care of you." Respect the traffic department [team that manages the agency's workflow], but remember they work for you, you don't work for them. Ask them for the briefs you want; tell me if you don't get them.

Get under the skin of a product and a brief. Don't show me work that the rest of the department might do. I don't need people to do what we already can.

Don't show it to me unless you like it or you think it's good. That's how I find out if you're good.

You're not here to solve a brief. You're here to be brilliant.

If you don't feel you can demonstrate your capabilities with the briefs we have, do it another way. Show me any idea for any brand on any problem.

Don't join the club; there isn't one. You're not here to make a load of friends and get to know the local pubs. You're unemployed, remember that. And, if you are any good you should be trying to make the rest of us look stupid.

If you put the effort into the work I'll put the effort into you and helping you.

But it works that way around. It's got to start with you.

Be confident, have faith in yourselves, work hard. Look after the work and the work will look after you. A placement is a moment in time. Seize it.

WHY PEOPLE WHO GET HIRED GET HIRED

The main reason people get hired is because they're good.

However, "good" on its own is not enough.

In the course of a year, a creative director will see many good teams. He can't hire all of them.

So what else do you need?

Luck. (When Napoleon was asked what was the most important quality in a general, he answered "lucky.")

For creatives, it's the same. Not even the agency's best teams do a good ad every single month. And yet if you are to impress the creative director, you may need to do a very good ad and you may only have a one-month placement to do it in. So you need luck. The right brief, at the right time.

But let's assume that you're good and you're lucky. Now all you need is for there to be a vacancy. Sometimes, a vacancy occurs because an agency is doing well—they win a big piece of business, more staff are needed…the placement team are on-site and doing good work; they get hired. On the other hand, sometimes a vacancy occurs because an agency is doing badly—the creative director needs to cut costs so he fires seniors and hires newbies.

So let's assume that you're good, you're lucky, and there's a vacancy. That should be enough. Except…it's rarely so clear-cut. The creative director may be convinced that you're good, but he may wonder if the next placement team might be even better. Or there may be a vacancy, but no pressing reason to fill it immediately, so the CD may be happy to let the situation slide.

There is no magic formula for getting hired.

SOME VARIABLES THAT MAKE A DIFFERENCE

However, over the years I have noticed a few variables that make a big difference.

The first is that teams who appear to be in demand are far more likely to get jobs. It's quite common to hear of teams on placement at an agency for several months, and doing well, but the creative director shows no inclination of wanting to hire them until they go into his office to tell him they're leaving, because they have a job offer from another agency. Now, of course, he offers them a job on the spot.

This is partly due to the arousal of his competitive instinct—his desire to "beat" the other agency. But it's mostly just regular human psychology, in that when we learn a commodity is in high demand, we automatically assume it to be more valuable. Even if the commodity is in reality identical today to what it was yesterday.

So don't be afraid to put yourself in the middle of a bidding war, if you can. Don't lie and say you've got a job if you haven't. Word gets around. But if you *have* been offered something elsewhere, even another placement or freelance work, make sure your current shop knows about it, as it may force their hand.

One quality that teams who get hired tend to have is they just "smell" like creatives.

Have you read *Blink* by Malcolm Gladwell? This wonderful book is all about the extraordinary power of "snap" judgements. We human beings tend to sum up a person or an object in an instant, and these instant appraisals have a surprising accuracy.

It turns out that the faculty this "blink" judgement relies on is memory. In other words, we run a comparison between the person or object in front of us, and all the similar ones we've encountered in the past.

That's why experienced CDs often claim they can tell "instantly" whether a young team are any good. It's not arrogance. They are simply mentally comparing the team in front of them with all the other young teams they have ever met. They know which of those previous young teams went on to be successful, so if the team in front of them seem similar, then they're a good bet.

Of course, the judgement is being made at an unconscious level. Which is why I compared it to a smell. It's an instinct. A feeling. A creative director might say *"there was just something about them"* or *"you could tell they were going to go far."*

I realize this doesn't help much. But it does at least explain.

Actually this leads on to my next point. Fitting in. We're getting into an area now that many people feel uncomfortable discussing. In fact, I probably get more heat on my blog about this than I do on any other subject.

Creatives seem to feel uncomfortable with the idea that the way they look has a bearing on how they are perceived (while simultaneously being utterly convinced that the "look" of an ad influences how a brand of margarine or soup is perceived).

I'll go into this subject in more detail in Chapter 9.

All I want to say for now is that you are more likely to be accepted into any group if the way you look and behave conforms to the norms of that group. Ad agencies are no different. I'm not advising you to change your haircut or your trousers, or suddenly start drinking a certain brand of beer or listening to a certain style of music. Far from it. Continue to be yourself. But just be aware that you are more likely to get hired somewhere you fit in. If you find yourself at an agency where you don't fit in at all, you are unlikely to get hired. Not a problem. Find somewhere else. There are all kinds of agencies out there.

CAN-DO

Make sure you display energy and a can-do spirit. I'm always impressed when I see that a creative team has got off their backsides and *done* something. (Remember—the word "create" means "to bring into existence" not "to ponder.") When my partner and I were going around with our student book, we had written one particular "spec" campaign (short for "speculative"—a campaign that you've mocked up for your book rather than one that has actually run), which people liked a lot. Creative teams were constantly telling us to make it happen for real. I couldn't understand why. Surely we should be judged on our ability to come up with good ideas, not our ability to organize a photoshoot? Eventually we gave in, and we made the thing come to life. Immediately, we noticed a huge difference in how we were perceived. The fact that we had "actually done it" got a great reaction from people—even though the campaign idea was identical to what it had been before, and the only difference was that it had actually been produced.

What I didn't realize at the time, but now know for certain, is that there is a lot more to being a successful creative than coming up with good ideas. Although there are many people in an agency who will help you bring your ideas to life, for example account handlers and TV producers, a can-do spirit on your part will be repeatedly important. And in making our campaign actually happen, we were displaying the initiative, energy, and can-do spirit that made people think we'd do well in a real job.

It's so easy nowadays to shoot a little ad on a camcorder, or print out some material for an ambient piece. Do it.

BEING AN INDIVIDUAL

One phrase you'll hear often is that *"creative directors are looking for people who offer something they don't currently have in the department."* This idea used to annoy the hell out of me. It was hard enough trying to master the "normal" disciplines such as TV commercials and posters—and now they wanted me to master some additional skill, specifically one that even the most experienced creatives in their department didn't have? And how was I supposed to know what skills the people in their department had anyway?

The answer is that they're looking for something that makes you an individual. At a job interview I had a few years ago, the creative director was more interested in my blog than he was in my book. No one in his department had a blog, and he found it fascinating. (Not many creatives had blogs at that time.) You shouldn't have to think too hard about this one. Everyone has something unique about them.

> *Everyone is either from an interesting place, has some weird or unusual hobby, or has done a weird or unusual job. Make something of it. Find a way to get it into your book if you can.*

Finally, I have a theory that every creative director is looking for a "dinner party story." Creative directors are regularly called upon to entertain—clients, new business prospects, even their own staff. And because they have repeated their good anecdotes hundreds of times, they constantly need new ones. Could you become his next anecdote?

I'm not saying you should deliberately set out to do something outrageous. (You can't create anecdotes, they have to occur naturally. A deliberate attempt to create an "incident" would be cringe-worthy.) But don't keep your head down during your placement and behave in a way that is completely boring and anonymous. Throw yourself fully into the agency's life and culture, and become not just another anonymous placement team but a real member of the agency, an individual with whom they've shared some history.

Jeremy Craigen

EXECUTIVE CREATIVE DIRECTOR
DDB LONDON, ENGLAND

What do you think are the most important qualities an advertising creative needs—above and beyond being able to write good adverts?

Naivety and optimism. You have to believe the client wants good work. You have to believe that even your worst clients are capable of buying good work. When your naivety ends at an agency, it's time to find another one.

What did you learn at college that helps you today?

I nearly trained to be an actor, but I wasn't good enough to get in to drama school! I've always loved ads and thought I would give that a try. I did the CAM course (Communications, Advertising and Marketing), which did nothing to help me get in to advertising but did make me realize I wanted to be a copywriter. I then did the D&AD advertising workshop where I met my first art director, Jeremy Carr, and then got a job at Ted Bates, a truly awful agency.

The main thing young teams want is simply a job. What are the behaviors and attitudes that make you want to hire a team? Why do some people get hired relatively quickly and others take longer…or maybe never get hired at all?

I only hire people who really want to work here. I only hire people who are talented and nice. I want to hire people who will challenge me with their work. Luck, of course, comes in to it. Right place at the right time, but you still have to have the above. Another thing I do is always ask myself the question "What does this team have that I don't already have in my department?"

What do you find is the hardest thing about being a creative, and what's the best thing?

The hardest part of being a creative is being consistently good. There are a lot of creatives out there who have done one nice thing but very few who have done, say, ten. The best part is, if you achieve this, then fame, fun, and fortune will follow.

Any tips for dealing with any of the other types of people that creatives come across, e.g. photographers or directors?

Work with the best people possible and let them do their job.

You first achieved success in the print medium, then later became successful in TV. Would you say that is a typical "progression," or do you think there are some teams who will always be "a good print team" or "a good TV team"?

I think there will always be some teams that are better in one discipline than another. I think it's easier to move from print to film than vice versa, as print people tend to be more idea-centric. You can make a great commercial without a great idea but not a great print ad.

During your time as executive creative director, DDB London has won massive hauls of awards at D&AD and Cannes. Is it therefore safe to assume that awards are important to you?

Awards are important to me, but they are not the be-all and end-all of what we do. Great work is. Unfortunately, the two don't always go together. All you can do is aim to do work you are proud of and hope that people on awards juries agree with you. Awards are a by-product of what we do. We are in the business of advertising, not winning awards. Having said all of that…you can't beat a week in Cannes!

You have worked at DDB for (at the time of writing) 18 years. Is there something to be said for loyalty? How come you haven't moved?

I have seen many changes here over the years; the agency is constantly evolving. I honestly can't think of anywhere else I'd rather work, even though I know I could go for more money (so loyalty isn't always rewarded…).

DDB is well known for the camaraderie that exists in the creative department, but some people claim our business is getting less fun than it was. Is that something you've noticed? Do you deliberately set out to make DDB a fun place to work?

I don't know if I deliberately set out to make DDB a fun place to work at. More a nice place to work. I always worry when I hear "it's not as fun as it used to be," because this never seems to come from the people producing great work. You're right about the camaraderie…though spiced with a healthy bit of competition.

Why do some creatives make it to creative director and others don't?

There are a lot of creatives out there and not many jobs as creative directors. Having said that, many creatives don't actually want to be CD. I certainly didn't when I was offered the job. The only reason I took it was I asked myself, "If I don't take it, who will?" I think, going back to your first question, that there are different qualities in a CD than a creative. Not just the usual leadership stuff but you have to be pragmatic, which is the last thing I want to see in a young team. You also have to revel in other people's success, something that doesn't come naturally to a creative.

CHAPTER 3
WHERE TO GET A JOB

There are many different kinds of advertising agencies.

The most significant difference is between the large shops, which tend to be part of an international "network" of agencies, and smaller ones, which service "local" business only, e.g. a "local" French agency means a firm that looks after brands that do not have a presence outside France, such as a French newspaper or department store chain.

It's important that you develop an understanding of what the different agencies are like, because you may end up working there for several years, so it's just as well to know what you're getting into.

DIFFERENT KINDS OF AGENCIES

NETWORK VERSUS START-UP

Let's talk first of all about the network agencies. These include names such as BBDO, DDB, TBWA, Saatchi, McCann, JWT, Ogilvy, Grey, Leo Burnett, Lowe, and Publicis. Each of these networks has agencies in many, many countries—in some cases that means 100 or even 150 offices. In turn, some of these networks are owned by giant "holding companies." For example, BBDO, DDB, and TBWA are all owned by Omnicom, a New York-based firm, which had revenues of more than $12 billion in 2007. That's a lot of dough.

These network agencies were built to service massive global brands. As you can imagine, it makes a degree of sense for a corporation like HSBC, a global bank operating in over 100 countries, to use an advertising agency that does too (at the time of writing, this is JWT).

If you like the idea of working on massive, famous brands like Ford, McDonald's, American Express, or Pepsi, then a network agency could be for you. These brands have hefty budgets to throw at their advertising; foreign shoots are common. The network agencies often have strong, deep, and long relationships with their clients, so their business is less volatile than that of a local agency, which may be heavily reliant on just two or three accounts (it's sometimes said that an ad agency is "never more than three phone calls away from disaster").

The trade-off for their stability is that these behemoths can be staid.

Some of them feel more like investment banks inside than they do advertising agencies.

No point being angry with them, however. The stakes are high if you are looking after an account that spends hundreds of millions of dollars a year. A cash cow like that gives birth to a lot of conservatism. And the opportunity to do radical work is arguably reduced if you are producing advertising that has to run in 50 or 100 countries.

However, it would be too simple to state it as inevitable that advertising's huge international corporations are more conservative than the young and hungry start-ups.

In fact, some of the world's most creative agencies are network agencies. Examples would be BBDO New York, Abbott Mead Vickers BBDO in London, TBWA Paris, and DDB London.

And whereas a few years ago there was a plethora of small creative start-ups all over the world, hungry to break the rules and produce stand-out work, a different business model has recently emerged—start-ups that produce mediocre, client-friendly advertising. Their true goal is not to be creative, but to make money for their founding partners when they sell their agency in five or ten years.

THE MICRO-NETWORK

In the last 20 years, a third agency model has emerged—the micro-network. Examples would be BBH and Wieden & Kennedy. These agencies aim to cover the world from a base of just one agency in each region, as opposed to one in each country. The idea is to have global scale and opportunities, but without the bureaucracy a network of 100+ offices can create.

IS THIS A COMPANY WHERE YOU CAN DO GOOD WORK?

AWARDS PER HEAD

What will affect you more than the agency's size is its ethos. If it's a local hotshop, are the founders keen to make their mark by doing truly outstanding work, or have they set up a cynical, profit-making enterprise? If international, is it a gray outpost of a gray global empire, or is it the flagship office of a network where creativity is part of their DNA?

In other words, what you need to know is—is this a company where you can do good work?

The easiest way to judge that is a measure I call Awards Per Head.

Of course, plenty of good work doesn't win awards, and plenty of poor or "scam" work does. Nevertheless, number of awards won is the only semi-objective measure of success that we have in our industry. And rightly or wrongly, awards are the most common yardstick used to judge a creative's merit. Nothing will help your career more than awards.

However, if you look only at the overall number of awards an agency has won, you could go wrong. You need to look at the ratio of awards to creatives. For example, let's say Agency A wins 30 awards a year, and Agency B wins 10. At first sight, Agency A is the better career choice. However, what if Agency A has 60 creatives and Agency B has only 10? In this case, although Agency A wins more awards, Agency B wins twice as many Awards Per Head, so if you take a job there you should have a better chance of winning awards.

I believe Awards Per Head is how all creatives rank agencies, albeit unconsciously. So it can't do any harm to be consciously aware of it, when deciding where you want to work.

There are other measures though. Ask yourself *"What portion of an agency's creative output would get you hired at that agency?"* If the answer is *"not much,"* then the portfolios of creatives at that agency are going *backwards*, year-on-year.

LOCATION, LOCATION, LOCATION

Age is a factor worth taking into account. Not the age of the agency—that makes no difference—but your own. If you are young and like to have fun, you may be drawn to an agency that's in a cool part of town, with young and good-looking staff, and funky décor. There's nothing wrong with that at all. You're living your life first; your career is just an aspect of your life.

On the other hand, if you are older, you may be drawn to an agency that is convenient for you to commute to, that is near good schools, or that offers a high level of job security. Same comment applies as in the previous paragraph.

You may start (or end) your career at an agency in a less fashionable city. Some countries—such as the US, Australia, and Germany—have more than one center of advertising excellence. In other countries—examples would be the UK, France, and Thailand—all the best agencies are concentrated in a single city. There are many advantages to working outside of the metropolis, however, in the so-called "regional" agencies. You'll often have a better standard of living and less pressure. On the other hand, you will have fewer creative opportun-ities, smaller budgets, and probably a smaller income. If you want to do great work, you will sooner or later have to move to where the great work is being done.

WHAT'S IN A NAME?

· Above-the-line (TV, print, and radio)
· Below-the-line (direct only)
· Through-the-line (everything from TV to point of sale)
· Integrated (same as through-the-line)

WHAT'S THE VIBE?

Also vital is the agency's style of work. Some agencies have strong styles, or philosophies, that you may be particularly drawn to (or repelled by).

Then there's the question of the media you want to work in. If you are a specialist in digital or direct, then you may want to work in an agency with that specialism. If you are a digital or direct specialist but are interested in expanding to other media, then it may be worth trying to get hired as a digital or direct team within a "traditional" agency. Once inside, you'll find the walls are pretty porous.

Advertising agencies are describing themselves with a confusing variety of terms nowadays. These include above-the-line (TV, print, and radio only), below-the-line (direct only), through-the-line (everything from TV to point-of-sale), and integrated (same as through-the-line). Some aren't even calling themselves advertising agencies; they are calling themselves 360-degree communications companies, brand content creators, or just ideas companies. In real terms, there's not much difference in how you go about getting hired at these different types of agencies, and they won't feel that much different once you're inside.

But the nuclear proliferation of buzzwords does make it hard for the poor creative to understand what is going on sometimes. It certainly means you have to do your research. Every company has a website, and every agency's website will feature a run-down of their work. Just make sure that, whatever they call themselves, the type of work they are actually doing is the type of work you want to do.

Some people have a theory that the secret of happiness is working somewhere you like the people. Others will tell you that the people are pretty much the same whatever agency you go to.

Whichever of those statements is true, it's undeniable that every ad agency has its own "vibe." The atmosphere, feel, or spirit of an agency depends on many factors. The most important is the personalities of the people in charge, since they make the decisions that shape the place.

Some agencies are funky environments—open-plan, with brightly colored furniture, the latest hip album blasting out...a pool table...maybe even a swimming pool if they're located somewhere warm.

Some are more austere. *"Yes, this place looks like sh*t but that's because all we care about is the work."*

It's pretty easy to get a feel for the vibe just by going into the agency and sitting in reception. When I was first looking for a job, my then-partner and I swore that you could tell everything you needed to know about an agency from its toilets. Marble toilets meant expensive but ultimately shallow advertising. Utilitarian toilets meant workmanlike advertising, and characterful toilets meant interesting work.

UP OR DOWN?

Another factor you should take into account is whether the agency is on the way up or the way down. There's no question that it's more fun and better for your career to work at an agency with *forward* momentum.

A shop that is still churning out the occasional good ad, but whose great days are some distance in the past, can be one of the most depressing of all places to work—where everyone lives in the past, complains constantly about the present, and may not have much of a future.

RATING THE CD

Another idea, which I have some sympathy with, is to choose an agency based on how you rate the creative director.

> *A good CD can improve an average agency quite quickly. But a creative director who is a politician, time-server, or "account man CD" can quickly turn a good agency into a slag-heap.*

Whether your CD rates *you* will have a huge effect on your likely success (the same goes for any boss, in any field). If you don't click at the interview you probably never will. If you already know him to be a royal pain in the arse, don't go to his agency hoping this won't matter, hoping you can just keep your head down and get on with the work. He'll get to you. I once spent a year at a small agency with a bad CD, and had to take two ibuprofen every afternoon—I was getting a headache every single day, without fail. The CD *was* that headache. He'd got to me.

MATTERS OF MONEY

Some agencies pay better than others. Usually, the best agencies don't pay the most. They don't have to—they know they can attract good staff by offering them the opportunity to do great work. But if you are in a situation or stage of your life where it's crucial that you maximize your income, then you may have to compromise on the quality of agency you work at. There's no shame in that.

Assuming you keep the quality of your work up, you can always make the reverse move later—trading down in money, and up in agency. Alternatively, you may decide you're happy at an agency where they pay well, and you don't have to bust your guts with all that cutting-edge creativity. That's fine too. Don't let other people's ideas of what you ought to do dictate what you do.

"Match your personality, goals, financial ambitions, and career-stage to the right agency." That, unsurprisingly, is the formula for career happiness. However, all this advice makes one rather large assumption—that you have a choice. But what if you don't have a choice? What if you can't get a job at the agency of your dreams? Should you take a job in a not-so-good agency, or tough it out until you *can* get hired somewhere great?

The answer is that it depends on your individual financial circumstances. If your internal organs are about to be called in by loan sharks, then obviously you have to take the job. But if you have some money squirreled away, or a cushy part-time job, then it's better to wait.

At the beginning of their careers, a lot of teams find they have to take a job working somewhere that isn't their ideal agency. And that's fine—plenty of great teams started in not-so-good agencies. The really important thing is what you do when you get there. Don't settle. Don't sit on your arse. If there's one good CD there, stick to them like a limpet and suck them dry for their knowledge. If there's one good account there, spend all your spare time working on that one account; it could be your ticket out. And spend the rest of your time on your spec book. When my partner and I were at a rubbish agency, we spent every night working on our book. Not once or twice a week. *Every night*. And some weekends too.

DON'T GET SUCKERED

If you are in a not-so-good agency, where the account teams are not able to sell good work, and the clients are not able to buy it, it's crucial that you make things happen for yourself. Every year at Cannes, a multitude of awards are won by creatives doing ads for dog obedience schools, toy model cars, anti-racism charities, and the like. Maybe it's not the highest ethical standards to pretend these were ads for real clients that actually ran, but at least those creatives are making the effort to put themselves in the shop window (more on these "scam" ads in Chapter 7).

The worst thing is to get comfortable in a bad agency.

It's easily done. There will be lots of nice people there, maybe a few good creatives, and a lot of people *talking* about doing nice work. But don't get suckered in. If the agency isn't regularly doing good work, then your career can't progress.

I knew one highly talented creative at college who was snapped up by one of the first agencies he saw. The agency never did good work, but they were lovely people and they liked my friend a lot. He started to do well there—learning to bury his creative ambition and do the kind of work they liked—and gradually earned a better and better living. After a few years, he was even put on the board. However, when the agency got taken over by another firm, and he was made redundant, he was unable to get another job *anywhere*, because he didn't have any good work to put in his portfolio. So someone who could have been a creative director at a top agency ended up leaving the industry.

If you do find yourself at a bad agency, stay focused on getting out. Because the vast majority of great work is done by the great agencies. And sooner or later, you want to get into one of those.

Flo Heiss

CREATIVE DIRECTOR
DARE, LONDON, ENGLAND

What do you think are the most important qualities an advertising creative needs—above and beyond being good at their job?

Be interested. Watch everything, read everything, listen to everything, eat, sleep, smell everything—be a sponge. Don't edit your life. Don't be a culture snob.

You studied extensively—in Augsburg, Urbino, and the Royal College of Art in London. What did you learn at college that helps you today?

I learned that I don't have the patience for a proper job such as a graphic designer.

Your agency puts a big effort into recruiting, via the Dareschool project. What are the behaviors and attitudes that make you want to hire a team? Why do some people get hired relatively quickly and others take longer...or maybe never get hired at all?

I am not interested in teams that have "wouldn't it be great if we did this…" type of ideas. I will hire teams that make big ideas happen. Teams that are daring and realistic at the same time. Admittedly they are as rare as Germans with a sense of humor. Also—make it absolutely clear which part of a campaign you were responsible for. I see so many portfolios from different teams with the same campaign in it. Be honest. I will find out. I know where you live.

Do you think certain types of people are more suited to certain types of agency… or should anyone be able to work anywhere?

I really don't know—I have been at Dare since 1876.

What's the hardest thing about being a creative, and what's the best thing?

The best thing is that you are always "on"—thinking about stuff. The hardest thing is that you can never switch off.

Everyone describes Flo Heiss as one of the "nicest" guys in the industry. Is it important for a creative to be nice?

You need to be able to tell someone in a nice way that their ideas are sh*t.

What is the right time to move agencies?

When you find an agency with that b2b account that no one wants to work on. Move in, make it yours. Or if your CD tells you in a nice way that your ideas are sh*t and you know he's wrong.

We work in a fun business. But some people claim it is getting less fun than it was. What do you think?

Consumers have become participants. The rules of advertising and marketing have changed. It is more difficult to create cut-through work that engages people. But if you crack a problem and your idea is flying round the globe it's more rewarding.

You are a prolific conference speaker, awards judge, and industry socializer. Is it important for creatives to "put themselves about"?

Talk to people, learn from your peers and heroes, but don't take yourself too seriously. It's only advertising.

Outside interests. Is it essential for a creative to love advertising, or is it healthier if their passions lie elsewhere?

I find creatives with a passion for advertising highly suspicious.

Do you think it makes a difference how a creative person looks or dresses, or does it not matter at all?

Of course it matters. Just look at my impeccable dress sense.

Why do some creatives make it to creative director and others don't?

Being a good creative doesn't automatically make you a good creative director. The clue is in the job title. A creative director needs to be able to spot a good idea in a pile of lameness and direct the creative to make it amazing. Some people have a natural ability to do this and some don't. (I nearly said the creative is the musician in an orchestra and the creative director is the conductor. I am glad I didn't because that's such a poor analogy.)

SURVIVING

CHAPTER 4
HOW TO WORK IN A TEAM

FINDING THE RIGHT PARTNER

It was Bill Bernbach (founder of DDB) who first put art directors together with copywriters, in the late 1950s, to make a two-person creative unit—a "team." It had never been done before, and it worked really well. Gradually everyone copied it. Most advertising agency creative departments in the world are now made up of teams.

In some countries, you can't even get a job unless you're part of a team. Colleges put their students into teams before they graduate, and agencies won't even see your portfolio unless you're part of a team.

(The US is a notable exception to this rule. In the US you can get hired to work in an ad agency whether you're a single, a team, or a kick-boxing troupe, as long as you're good.)

Most people find their partner at college. Good reason to go to college. On most courses, you have the opportunity to work with a wide variety of people. On the course I took, there were 30 of us, of whom 15 were art directors. I got to work with all 15 of them. That was great, because you get an idea of what kind of partnership suits you.

Finding a partner isn't as daunting as it sounds. Like any other relationship in life, chemistry is crucial. You know quickly whether it's going to fly. When I first met my partner, we didn't stop talking for a fortnight. We were gabbling away, talking about advertising, talking about strategies, each trying to impress, perhaps, but for sure we got on like a magnet and a fridge.

But if you do leave college without a partner, it's no disaster. Many headhunters carry lists of "singletons," which they'll let you have without charge. You should also work your contacts—you will have made a few industry contacts by this point—and let everyone from your course know. In fact, tell *everyone* you know…even the people who aren't in advertising. They may know someone who is. Look under every stone. Someone will turn up.

Having a partner is an uncommon thing in the world of work. But it's great. You've always got someone to talk to at parties. You have someone to bounce ideas around with. And as someone without a partner told me the other day, it stops the voices.

My partner and I have been together, at the time of writing, for 12 years. Most of them miserable of course, but nevertheless, it's lasted.

It's often said that a creative partnership is like a marriage. And it is. Except you'll probably see more of your partner than you will of your spouse. And you don't have sex with them. Or you shouldn't, anyway.

So you have to make sure it's the right person.

DOES IT FEEL RIGHT?

Trust your instincts. Don't "talk yourself into" a partnership. If it doesn't feel right, it isn't. If you've been single for a while, you may be tempted to take a partner just because you need a partner. As with the romantic kind of partner (yes, this metaphor never runs dry) it just isn't the right thing to do.

Similarly, don't team up with someone just because they're already in a job or a placement. The instant leg-up could turn into a long-term nightmare if you're not compatible. And don't assume that just because someone is already in a job or has more experience than you then they "must be good." They may not be. Make sure you judge the person, not their situation—the situation will change, the person won't.

As with all relationships, don't leap straight in. If possible, work together for a trial week or two, and see how it goes (agree that upfront; it's more professional).

And don't be embarrassed to check them out. Google them. Talk to people who know them. What's their reputation? Were they being carried by their previous partner? Are they a psycho?

DIFFERENT BUT NOT THAT DIFFERENT

The conventional view of a well-suited team is that it's two people who get on well, have a similar view of advertising, and share the same goals.

However, you must, must, must find someone who thinks a bit different to you. There's no point having two people in the room who think the same way. If that's the case, why have two?

The classic example of a well-balanced team has one person who thinks visually and another who is more verbal (the art director/copywriter combination). But it doesn't have to be split that way. It used to be said that a great comedy-writing duo comprised one writer and one pacer. Some creative teams seem to have a "front-man" and a "quiet one," which may correspond to "one thinker and one talker." But it doesn't matter. Just as long as your temperaments, psyches, or spheres of reference are somehow different.

On the other hand, you must find somebody you have quite a bit in common with. If you are a 36-year-old male from Manchester, and your partner is a 21-year-old female from Moscow, then you are going to have big problems. You are going to say *"We could art direct it in the style of the Clangers"* and she is going to say *"What is this Clangers?"*

It helps if you find them a bit funny. Whether you laugh *with* them or *at* them doesn't matter. As long as there's some humor there.

Find someone who has the same level of commitment. In other words, if you want to work Christmas Day, find someone else who wants to work Christmas Day. And if you are laid-back, find a partner who is equally so. A mismatch here and you're in trouble. The most successful British team of the 1990s was Tom Carty and Walter Campbell. The story of how they partnered up is illuminating: they were constantly running into each other in their creative department's kitchen, making coffee at 10.30pm. Everyone else had gone home. Including their respective partners.

Look for someone you find interesting. You are going to have to sit opposite them for upward of nine hours a day. You are going to have to take airplanes with them, sit in edit suites and soulless conference rooms with them. Pick someone who says something interesting now and again.

Oh, and you've got to rate their work.

WORKING WELL WITH YOUR PARTNER

The basics are the same as any human interaction. You need to listen to each other, respect each other's point of view, and not expect the other to be perfect. After all, *you're* not.

Agree between you exactly what the brief is about before you start writing ads. There's nothing more frustrating than your partner spending two hours drawing pictures of snakes having slightly misheard that vital briefing on snails.

If they write a nice headline, or come up with a good visual, tell them. Sounds obvious I know, but we're all praise-whores in this business, aren't we? Your partner is no exception.

Constantly be sharing information with your partner. It's amazing how often a crucial conversation takes place while one of you is in the toilet. Make sure you tell them as soon as they get back.

Be aware of each other's strengths and weaknesses. If your partner hates presenting work, don't make him. If you're no good at speling, get your partner to check your copy.

There will be times when you carry him, and times when he carries you. Don't worry about this. It is normal. Only if you have been carrying him for a period longer than about six months do you need to have "a chat."

Have regular conversations about *"what we want to achieve this year"* and *"where do we see our careers heading."* The boat will go better when you're both rowing in the same direction.

In general, you should only present ideas that both of you like. It's the easiest way to narrow down your pile. But if he is desperate to present an idea that you absolutely hate, let him. My partner and I call it *"playing a joker."* The main reason to do it is that it avoids an argument, which, because it can't be resolved, will waste time and could get heated. Also, you don't want him to feel his creativity is being stifled. The resentment could block him up for half a day. So, even though every fiber of your being is telling you that his idea is an embarrassment, let it go forward. What's the worst that can happen? If the idea doesn't get bought, you can tell him *"I told you so."* If the idea does get bought and is brilliant, you will share the credit. You can't lose.

LONELY HEARTS

Art director seeks copywriter for long term relationship. GSOH essential. Must enjoy strategy meetings and ambient advertising. Dislikes: account directors.

HOW TO DISAGREE NICELY

Here is a real discussion between two creatives, overheard through a wall.

CW: It's sh*t.

AD: What do you mean it's sh*t?

CW: I mean that it's sh*t.

AD: But why is it sh*t?

CW: It's sh*t because it's sh*t, that's all.

Yes, this is what it's like for everyone. Don't worry about it.

Most of our job consists of discussing ideas. And because this activity is entirely subjective—there's no Excel spreadsheet that can determine whether an idea is right or not—and because (as previously discussed) 99 percent of all ideas will be rejected, and because (as previously discussed) the two people in the room do not think the same way about everything—it's inevitable there will be disagreement.

And if you feel passionately about an advert—you're in the wrong business if you don't—there will be times when those disagreements become arguments. I know of one creative who, in the heat of a row, stabbed his partner in the leg with a scalpel. That's probably going too far.

Nevertheless, it's not good working practice to suppress debate. Let disagreements be aired, else one partner can be left with resentment. It's OK to argue. A creative partnership is one long argument!

And how you handle that continuous process of debate will determine how successful you are as a team.

SAYING YES NOT NO

The best technique for discussing ideas is the one that is sometimes announced at the beginning of brainstorming sessions. (Hateful word, brainstorming.) The moderator normally begins these sessions by instructing participants not to use the word "no," but instead to be exclusively positive, because it's too early in the process to rule anything out—at this stage they are just looking for potential, and every idea has potential. That last part is nonsense of course. However, the deeper utility of the principle is that people hate being told "no." It may cause them to become angry, withdrawn, or unco-operative. This can even apply to someone you've worked with for years, if they happen to be in a bad mood that day. So I recommend applying the (hateful word) brain-storming principle to your own daily routine.

The simplest way to operate is that instead of saying "no," you simply say "yes" in an unconvinced tone of voice. Sounds basic, but it really works. You will avoid hours and hours of arguments. As I've said, I have nothing against arguments. But they should come from genuine disagreement about the work, not from one-upmanship or bruised ego.

You should never disagree with anything your partner says in a meeting, even if it could get them carried away by the men in white coats. You've got to be a united team, otherwise account handlers, directors, or whoever you're dealing with, will decide that this team doesn't know what it's doing, and will simply make the decisions themselves. You don't want that to happen. So any disagreements you may have, sort out behind closed doors.

In general, avoid long debates. Time is your only resource. By all means tell your partner that an idea has already been done, is illegal, or is off-brief, but don't spend 20 minutes trying to kill it while he tries to defend it. That's a waste. Just move on, and use those 20 minutes to have a better idea instead.

Here are some other discussion techniques that may help prevent rows:

WHAT YOU WANT TO SAY	HOW TO SAY IT
· Good, but I think we can do better.	· Good.
· Hmmm. Strategically sound, but not interesting.	· Yes, that works (neutral tone).
· Interesting, but strategically unsound.	· Interesting (neutral tone).
· There may be something good in there, but right now it doesn't work at all.	· Interesting—worth developing.
· Off-brief, and pretty dull.	· Uh-huh (neutral tone).
· Wildly off-brief.	· Say that one again?
· Still wildly off-brief.	· OK, I get it now.
· Incredibly boring.	· OK.
· Rambling, dull, and uninspiring.	· Shall we break for lunch?

A good rule of thumb for resolving arguments is to let the copywriter have final say on headlines, dialogue, and suchlike; and the art director on photographers, images, and suchlike.

Another is to let the person who feels most passionately about the issue, win.

IT'S A KIND OF MARRIAGE

Don't go to bed on an argument. Always listen to your partner's point of view. Remember their birthday. And don't look at other art directors in the street.

Just as there are many types of successful marriages, there are many different types of successful creative partnerships. So don't worry if other teams seem to do things differently to you, like work longer or shorter hours than you do, have more or fewer arguments, socialize with each other outside work or don't, drink or don't drink at lunchtime. All that matters is if your relationship works for you.

In the end, the proof of a good partnership is the ideas that come out of it.

RELATIONSHIP PROBLEMS

When things aren't going well, and you're feeling frustrated, it's a natural tendency to blame your partner. Well, you're hardly going to blame yourself, are you?

But in my experience, teams that are getting great work out are rarely unhappy. Most teams that are unhappy are teams who are not currently producing good work. In other words, what you may think is a relationship problem may be some other kind of problem. Perhaps the agency isn't doing well. You're not working on good accounts. Or you've just had bad luck.

Don't be too quick to blame your partner, since your problems may be the problems of you both, not just his. Also, never forget that if you are feeling frustrated, the most likely cause is not any inadequacy of your partner's, but the fact that you work in a frustrating job. A job where you spend the whole day making wonderful creations that other people stomp on. The best stratagem for dealing with that is to go to the gym, chill out with a movie, pour yourself another glass of whatever you can find in the fridge, have a good old bitch to your wife/girlfriend/boyfriend. That's what they're there for.

A common complaint is people feeling they're "carrying" their partner. Beware. We all think our own ideas are great. If you feel strongly that you are carrying a passenger, make sure you do an *objective* check on that. Go through all the ideas that you and your partner have had approved by creative directors in the last two years (not client-approved; too many random factors go into that), and see if you really are laying more eggs than he is. Remember to adjust for role differences. In other words, if your partner is the art director, and spends a lot of time on shoots or in the studio, then he can't be expected to come up with as many ideas as you. If your partner is the copywriter, he should be coming up with more than you do.

If there's a problem, talk about it. Not at the time, when you're angry, because that will only lead to bloodshed, but later—when you can both be reasonable. If talking becomes hard, use some other channel. One creative team that I know is incapable of discussing any "relationship issues" face-to-face, but they have an understanding that they can text each other about them. A CD of my acquaintance recommends you have a monthly lunch with your partner, and get hammered together. That way, any issues are sure to come out, rather than fester.

Over the course of your career, you will inevitably come to a point at least once—probably more than once—when you want to make a change. Sometimes it will happen naturally, without you doing anything. If you're not getting on well, it may be because you have different goals, and his different goals may take him in a different direction career-wise, or to a different city or country. You could try doing nothing for a few months, and see if that happens of its own accord.

Only break up with your partner as a last resort. Remember, you will be dumping the devil you know.

BREAKING UP

If you're not doing good work together, not enjoying each other's company, not talking, constantly feeling frustrated with them, let down by them, or contemptuous of them...then it's time to break up.

There are as many horror stories surrounding the dumping of a partner as there are around the dumping of a girl- or boyfriend.

One copywriter went on holiday, and when he got back, he found someone else sitting in his chair.

I could tell the story of the time I got dumped. My art director went on a road-trip around the US, and simply never called me when he got back. Good holiday was it, Al?

I've dumped once and been the dumpee once. So I have experience of both sides of the fence.

The first point to make is a practical one. If you want to break up with your partner, it's down to you to go and get another job. They get to stay. You don't. That's just the way it is. (Again, the analogy is with a marriage. If you are the one who wants to leave the marriage, then it is you who must leave the marital home.)

At least have the courage and decency to tell them in person. However, you shouldn't tell them that you want to break up until you have a concrete offer to go somewhere else. Don't pointlessly destabilize the team by saying you're breaking up, and then not doing anything about it. In other words, it's better to find another partner before you break up with your current one. That may sound mercenary, but the purpose of it is to avoid limbo and uncertainty, which aren't good for either of you.

And most of all, if you are certain that the relationship has run its course, then don't be afraid of anything.

Don't be afraid of what the future may hold. If you are good at your job, you will be fine.

Don't be afraid of having to look for a new partner. It can be done. Thousands have done it.

(On the other hand, don't be afraid of going through hard and difficult conversations with your current partner. You may be able to fix things. Thousands have done this too.)

Just don't do nothing.

TOP FIVE VALID REASONS FOR BREAKING UP WITH YOUR PARTNER

1 Different goals. You want to work in different countries or different cities. Or, one of you wants to do great work, while the other wants an easy life.
2 Your ideas are too different—you can never agree on anything. (Or alternatively, they're too similar —no point having two of you in the room.)
3 Your personal relationship has irretrievably broken down.
4 Relationship has gone stale; time for a new challenge.
5 Ability mismatch. In other words, you think you're brilliant, and they're rubbish. (Funnily enough, it's never the other way round....)

Siimon Reynolds

FOUNDER
THE PHOTON GROUP, AUSTRALIA

You have a wide variety of interests—anti-ageing, personal development, meditation, kung fu...do you believe it's healthier for an advertising creative to have passions outside the world of advertising, or is it OK to be obsessed purely with the ad business?

You have to have both. I've not seen anyone excel in advertising who didn't have intense focus on it. Warren Buffett was once asked what was the biggest single factor behind his success—he said "focus." When people get too interested in other areas, their advertising then doesn't reach the highest level. On the other hand, you need an escape valve. Also, creativity is like a library. If you keep taking books out and don't put any in, you eventually won't have any books left. And if you're too insular, you'll end up producing formula work, which just looks like it's from old D&AD annuals. Why did Crispin Porter move to Colorado? I think it was about getting new influences. So you need both.

What do you think are the most important qualities an advertising creative needs—above and beyond being able to write good adverts?

They need to live in the future. They need to see themselves as great advertising people before they actually are. You need to have that self-image, and then work towards becoming it. If you see yourself as a junior writer, you will be. Envision your future self. Pump yourself up. There's so much failure in our business. Our life is all about rejection; you have to really work on your self-belief. You also need good time-management skills. Creatives waste a colossal amount of time during the day, and then work too-long hours in the evening. Also, you need to have a learning mind-set. After a time, people stop learning. They start to coast. The greats don't—David Abbott won a Gold One Show Pencil at the age of 60. And treat it like a profession, not an artform. Many creatives get thrown by the joviality in the business, and spend a lot of time going to the pub. They don't realize that the people at the top only got there because they were dedicated. As Dave Trott says: "energy displaces talent."

Whenever I've seen you in photographs or videos, you're always smartly dressed. Was that something you did from the beginning? Do you think it makes a difference how a creative person looks or dresses, or does it not matter at all?

Only a shallow person doesn't judge by appearances! I used to have super-long hair in my 20s. That meant I had to do a lot of work with some clients, to get them to treat me as an equal. I believe in dressing for the job above you. If you want to be a creative director, dress like your CD.

What did you learn at college that helps you today?

I never went to college. I started in advertising straight from school, though I did later do a ten-week program run by AWARD in Australia, which was good. I'm a little suspicious of three-year advertising courses. What kind of unhelpful stuff must they be teaching, to fill three entire years?

TOMORROW'S GREATS

Australian

You have a high media profile—even appearing on the Australian version of the *Dragons' Den* TV show. Did you make a deliberate decision to build your profile? Do you think it's an important skill for creatives to learn?

What happened with me was entirely circumstantial. I had become a CD very young—aged 21—and that created a story for journalists. Then once you get quoted a few times, you keep getting contacted, again and again. Because journalists read other journalists. So, I didn't actively pursue it. But it is very beneficial if you can create a profile. People believe journalists. If you can get good stuff written about you, it will really help you, for example, in terms of getting hired for senior jobs.

Do you think creatives could benefit from being more business-minded?

Absolutely. David Abbott once said: "Think like a creative, and talk like an accountant." The typical creative's self-image is "artist," whereas it should be "enabler for commerce." A lot of creatives get to creative director and they've never read the *Financial Times*. They're babes in the wood when it comes to commerce. That's part of what creates disrespect for advertising people.

FINANCIAL REVIEW

THE DAILY HABIT OF SUCCESSFUL PEOPLE.

DON'T
BE AN
INCOMEPOOP.

You have started your own agency, more than one in fact, and had phenomenal success. What advice would you give to a creative thinking of doing a start-up?

The reason companies start is because someone who is good at a craft (say copywriting) thinks they can run a business. But what you need to have a successful business are discipline, order, and structure. They are very different to the skills you need to be a creative. So you must either learn to be entrepreneurial, or find partners who are. A lot of people underestimate the hardship and pain and lack of money from starting their own agency. People who don't really, really want to run their own business would probably be better off as CDs in a network agency.

We work in a fun business. But some people claim it is getting less fun than it was. What do you think?

The whole of business has become more efficient. So a lot of slack has gone, for sure. But what I would say is be your own microcosm. What's that song—"Everywhere you go, you always take the weather?" Be a center of fun and positivity. You don't want your work to become boring. To be successful, you have to be playful and daring. I'll never forget a shot I once saw of Diego Maradona in a training session. He was executing a phenomenal scissor-kick... and his laces were undone. Now, the average person would say "do up your laces, or you're going to trip over." But the expression on his face was pure joy and exuberance. So don't ask if the business is fun. Ask *"am I fun?"*

When is the right time to get out of advertising?

Always give it 100 percent, even if you want to leave. Otherwise your work will get worse, and you'll just become mediocre. When should you get out? When you've got the finances to do the next thing you want to do.

CHAPTER 5
HOW TO SELL
YOUR WORK

GET REFERENCE

When you come up with an idea, you probably have a picture in your head of what you want the finished piece of work to look like. But to sell it to others—your creative director, the account team, the client—it's essential that you get "reference": images or film clips that will help *them* see it.

Of course, there's a danger that if you show people reference of something similar to your idea, they'll conclude that what you're proposing is not original. For that reason, you should only ever be producing reference for an executional style or technique, never for a strategy or an idea. There's a big difference, because taking a style from one artform and applying it to a completely different arena can produce something that feels totally original. But starting with an unoriginal idea will always produce unoriginal work, however you dress it up.

Not everyone needs to see reference—some of the people you present your ideas to are perfectly capable of visualizing from a script or a scamp. But many aren't. There are lots of people in this business who are great at marketing or strategy or account handling, but who couldn't visualize a red bottom unless you show them a picture of somebody being spanked. (This doesn't make them bad people, incidentally. They just need your help.)

The importance of helping them see it is that if people don't know what your ad is going to look like, they might not realize how good it is, so they might not like it as much as they should, so they might fail to sell it (account team) or buy it (client).

GET THEM TO SEE IT YOUR WAY

Even if they *do* buy it, the fact that you haven't fully explained what it's going to look like means everyone will start visualizing it in their own individual way, and might want it executed their way. You don't want that. You want it your way. Also, once people have formed their own picture of something, it can be hard to get them to change it. This will cause arguments further down the line; the kinds of arguments that steal time and sap your energy.

Of course, you don't want to spend hours and hours collecting reference for a route, only to watch your creative director blow the whole thing out in 30 seconds. So start small. You may start with just an image, for presentation to your CD, and then step up the amount of reference you show as the process goes along. But you certainly don't want to start too late. Some creatives only look for reference when an idea is just about to go to the client. I think that's a mistake. John Webster, perhaps the greatest-ever British creative, never showed an idea to anybody—even the lowliest account handler—without reference. From the very beginning of the process, he made people "see it"—and he made them see it his way.

Nick Gill, the executive creative director at BBH in London, who is generally thought of as one of the UK's best writers of TV commercials, often presents his TV scripts along with the *music track* that he has in mind for the ad. It's amazing to what extent the "right track" helps people to understand his idea, brings it alive for them, and makes them like it more.

Nick sometimes draws his own storyboards too. He often has a movie scene that he'll play people as a reference. And he's not afraid to act his ads out to the room. Compare that with the typical creative, who simply reads out the script in a flat monotone—or even just hands it over and asks people to read it for themselves. Nick understands that it's difficult for people to "buy" a mere script on a page. So he doesn't ask them to. Instead, he does anything he can to bring his script to life. It's no wonder he gets so many of his ideas made.

Top: This is what a typical "scamp" looks like—a simple black-and-white line drawing that explains the concept.
Bottom: And here is the finished ad.

PRESENTING TO THE CREATIVE DIRECTOR

The way a creative presents his work should vary according to whom he's presenting—clients like a lot of fluff and preamble, account teams a little bit, creative directors don't like any. I mean it—nada.

Why? Because the first thing to remember about presenting to your creative director is that he is short of time. His day consists of meetings, a sandwich, and then more meetings. His Blackberry pings ceaselessly. Everyone in the agency needs his opinion, his approval...I have seen account handlers follow a CD into the toilet to get time with him.

So the biggest favor you can do your creative director is to make things quick.

That means no preamble.

All you do is remind him which brief you've come to show work on. That's important. Because while *you've* been working on this solidly for a while, and it's uppermost in your mind, *he* might not have given it a thought since he signed the brief off two weeks ago; he may not even know what you're here for.

So you walk in and say: *"Hi, Steve. We're here to see you about Toyota, that 'reliability' radio brief for the Camry."*

You mention which brief it is, and maybe what the proposition was, just to focus his mind, but that's it.

Don't go through an explanation of why the work you've done is right. The consumer won't get an explanation before he sees the work; your CD doesn't want one either. All he wants is to see the work. Nothing else.

HOW?

So how should you present that work?

As simply as possible. If it's a TV script, an old cheat is to write what the idea is at the top of the page. That makes it easier for him. If it's print, have it simply drawn up, or Mac-ed up, if necessary. If it's digital, put it in whatever form comes across most clearly. Remember—the quicker an idea is to "get," the more people think it's good. Don't forget to bring reference (though if you're presenting several ideas, you wouldn't be expected to have reference for all of them).

But whatever you do, don't use PowerPoint. Not that there's anything wrong with PowerPoint; there's actually a lot of cool stuff you can do with it. But if a creative tried to, he would probably be carted off to the loony bin. Why, I don't know; after all, it's just words and pictures. Nevertheless, the use of PowerPoint in creative circles is considered actively evil. So do not learn how to use it, and if for some reason you already have learned it, unlearn it. Fast.

WHEN?

As you can see, *how* you present to your creative director is a matter of the utmost simplicity. The trickier question is *when* you present.

Do you wait until you have an idea that you would die on a sword for?

Or do you go in when you have four or five ideas that you like, and rely on him to pick out the best one—after all, "that's his job?" Or do you go in with "a few thoughts," and aim to work with him collaboratively, to turn one of them into something good?

I remember one boss I had, years ago, telling me *"I want you to run in."* By which he meant *"don't show me any work until you've got something so exciting you just physically can't hold yourself back from sprinting into my office."*

He hadn't taken on board that his title—creative director—implied he should be giving the creatives some direction, rather than just waiting for them to come in with the answer. But to be fair, that kind of laziness is rare. After all, if every team could get to the answer without help, then there would be no need for creative directors, and he wouldn't have a job.

At the other end of the scale is the "bring me your wounded, bring me your lame" attitude—in other words, show me anything you've got, and let's see if we can make it work. Apparently David Droga tries to see all of his teams every day. His attitude is that as a creative, time is your only resource. And he doesn't want his creatives wasting any. He doesn't want them working for more than 24 hours on a thought he might not like; he'd rather see all their half-thoughts than one or two finished ones.

So the answer on when to present depends on the attitude of your creative director. Every CD is different. You need to learn—as quickly as possible—whether he likes to see a lot of ideas, or whether he prefers that you do more culling first.

If you are getting too many insults—creative directors specialize in the finely honed insult—then this is a clue that you are going in too early. (We once showed something to Jeremy Craigen when I was at DDB and he said: *"That is a really good ad...for Publicis Bratislava, maybe."*)

As a general rule, the more experienced the team, the fewer ideas you should be showing, because you should have a better idea yourself of what is good. Therefore, young teams should go in with several ideas. Young creatives often have great ideas that they don't know are great, because they don't have the experience to recognize it. So go in early, go in often, go in with anything you've got that's coherent, draw stuff up clearly but not beautifully, and don't invest hours crafting dialogue. After all, you don't want to spend days buffing up your gem only to be told by your CD that you've been polishing a turd.

PRESENTING TO THE TEAM

By "the team" I mean account handlers, planners, engagement planners...anyone at the agency who works on the account you've been briefed on.

By way of example, let's look at how a well-known campaign idea might hypothetically have been presented. Bear in mind I have no clue how Tom Carty and Walter Campbell, the creatives at AMV.BBDO in London who created "Good Things Come To Those Who Wait" for Guinness, actually did present it, and I've never met either of them so I'm no doubt completely misrepresenting their personalities. But I like to think the meeting went something like this...

BRIGHT AND BREEZY

Tom and Walt: *"Morning all. Hi! Come on in. Everyone got a seat? Great."*

The point to notice here: Tom and Walt have begun the selling of their idea before the team even sits down.

Tom and Walt have adopted a bright and breezy manner. They are friendly and open. Do they particularly like this account team? Maybe, maybe not. But they understand the importance of projecting confidence. They understand that at this crucial moment—the first presentation of an idea—the account team will be scanning every sound and gesture that they make.

You see, the account team has spent weeks or months developing this brief, and they have had endless conversations with the clients and the creatives about it. Finally they are about to see the result. Their curiosity is rampant. And what they basically want to know is one thing—have the creatives cracked it? Have the creatives produced something they believe in; something the account team should believe in; something the whole agency should get behind; something that might be a career-changing piece of advertising for everyone who comes into contact with it? Admittedly, that's more likely for the next Guinness ad than it is for, say, a small-space print ad for a trade publication. But even with the smallest ad, there are stakes. If it hasn't been cracked, the account team may be facing a world of pain.

Accordingly, if you have cracked it, be confident. Signal it. If you haven't cracked it, and this is going to be a playing-for-time meeting, then signal that too. Start with a frown and a sigh. Manage their expectations. Tell them that you don't think you've cracked it, but you've got something that may start an interesting discussion. Tell them you've got more questions than answers at this point. And then do actually have lots of questions. Convince them you have the desire and the energy to crack it next time. Otherwise, the next time they come in, they walk in hostile.

THE PREAMBLE

Tom and Walt: *"As you'll remember, the brief was all about how Guinness has more substance than lagers do. It's even reputed to have health benefits."*

This is what we call a preamble. Account teams don't like ideas to be presented cold; it makes them uncomfortable. They love to start the presentation with a quick recap of the brief. And this seemingly meaningless ritual does in fact have an important purpose—by demonstrating to the team that you have been working to the correct brief, you are providing vital reassurance, and making an advance claim about the saleability of your idea. Both good things.

The preamble puts the account team in a reassured and receptive state, and the state we are in when we receive information has a crucial bearing on how we perceive that information. By contrast, creatives who hand over a script and stare at their shoes will not sell as many scripts.

This may sound like a lot of effort for the benefit of the account team, who after all aren't the ultimate buyers of the work. But it's worth it. The more you can get the account team to buy into your route, the harder they will sell it to the client.

Notice in the example above how clever Tom and Walt were in their preamble. When recapping the brief, they subtly highlighted the one aspect of it they addressed in their work.

This "reframing" of the brief is a fantastically useful maneuver. For planners, it's essential, but it's also a great skill for creatives to master. The principle is that, since few ideas are exactly 100 percent on brief, you slightly reframe the brief just before you present the work, so the work seems like it matches the brief more closely than it really does.

Tom and Walt: *"We've come up with this endline—Good Things Come To Those Who Wait."*

N.B. They haven't handed over the script yet.

Tom and Walt: *"The campaign's all about waiting. The idea is that a pint of Guinness is substantial and therefore worth waiting for, just as all good things in life are worth waiting for."*

It really pays to literally start one sentence of your presentation with "The idea is..."

We creatives are experts at extracting the idea instantly from a script. Many account handlers and planners are too, but by no means all. However, they all know how crucial "the idea" is; so make sure you tell them what it is.

Tom and Walt: *"I've got to tell you, we're very excited about this. Abbott loves it."*

Sell, sell, sell, baby. One of the most successful commercials directors of the last 20 years—a guy called Tarsem—sold cars in L.A. to fund his way through film school. You don't have to do that. But if you're asking the team to commit the next six months of their lives to something, you should at least be able to tell them you're excited about it.

Tom and Walt: *"Now, we've got this script about a group of guys—they're surfers—and they're waiting for the perfect wave. See what you think."*

And only now do they hand the script over. That's right. A full two-and-a-half minutes of preamble. That's not too much to ask, is it?

Even better than handing the script over—read it out, if you have acting skills. If it's a print ad, talk them through the imagery. If it's a digital idea, tell them what's cool about it.

So to sum up, presenting to the team is really no big deal (although a lot of young creatives seem terrified of it). You just explain what the idea is, and why it's on brief, and hand it over. But don't wang on.

PRESENTING TO THE CLIENT

Should creatives present their work to the client? This is one of the most vexed questions in advertising. In some countries, such as the US, it is standard practice that creatives present their own work. In other countries, such as the UK, they almost never do. British creatives are stunned when they find out that American creatives do all the presenting. *"So what do the account handlers do?"* they ask.

If your agency has a firm policy on whether creatives present their work or not, then this section will be irrelevant to you, since you will be obliged to follow that policy.

However, in many countries, and in many agencies, the question remains unresolved.

There are agencies where some of the creatives present to clients and others don't. There are agencies where the creatives present on certain accounts and not on others. It's a gray zone.

But if you have the choice, what should you do?

IN FAVOR OF CREATIVES PRESENTING

The main argument in favor of presenting your own work is that the passion a creative shows can win a client over. As it's your work, you're going to be utterly convinced it is good, and conviction can be highly persuasive.

Not only will you feel more passionately about the work than an account handler can, but as it's your idea, you'll be able to bring it to life with more vividness and precision, which should mean a higher chance of a sale.

There's even a theory that presenting your own work saves time, because you'll be able to deal with any objections on the spot, rather than entering into a back-and-forth via the account handler.

And maybe you should ask yourself—if it's not worth your time to take a cab across town and stand up for your work…are you sure it will be worth the next four months of your time that it will take to produce it?

BUILDING A RELATIONSHIP WITH THE CLIENT

Looking beyond this one sale, there's a chance that by presenting directly to a client you can start to build a relationship with them that could prove fruitful for the future, and open a channel of communication that is clearer and more direct, because it's not mediated through the filters of the account handlers and planners.

When you meet clients, you have to behave differently to how you behave within the agency—you have to understand that, to them at least, advertising is a serious business activity. James Cooper, creative director of Dare New York, complains:

"Too many creatives behave like it's a game. They try to see how far they can take the game. In other words 'What can we get away with—with the clients' money?' Short-term this is great fun, 'Hey, it wasn't a great ad but we got to go to Cape Town again,' but long-term the client will think you are an immature idiot. The easiest way to get great work out is to form a proper long-term relationship with a client—do not assume that's someone else's job."

You are certainly going to have to develop "client-facing" skills one day, when you become a creative director. That is why some believe that the sooner you meet clients, the better. There's an argument that rank-and-file creatives are the most disposable individuals in an agency, because of their lack of client relationship. If a creative vanishes overnight (because the agency needs to reduce overheads), no client is any the wiser, whereas an agency has to think twice before getting rid of an account person or a planner, because they have to consider "the relationship."

On the other hand, being able to present effusively has made the career of many a hack. We all know the type. They wax loudly and enthusiastically about the client's product during meetings. They present awful scripts, with much bravado and theatricality—the hack is often a fine actor—scripts they swear will make the client "famous." The client is blown away that anyone is that zealous about their product—far more zealous than they are themselves—and the hack quickly becomes their favorite creative and number-one go-to person. And thus, a career is born. Albeit an undeserving one.

If your presentation skills exceed your talent, then maybe this is a valid path to pursue.

AGAINST CREATIVES PRESENTING

Despite what I have just said, I am a firm believer that creatives should not present their work to clients, if they have the choice.

Most account people are more charming and more articulate than most creatives. So why have the creatives do the presenting? It doesn't make sense. I am a huge fan of getting people to do what they're best at. You wouldn't ask a striker to play in goal, would you? And if you're appearing in court, you would want a professional advocate to put your case for you, rather than presenting it yourself, I am sure.

The account person knows the client better than you do, so may know better how to sell to him, and how to meet his objections—account handlers are experienced at resisting the onslaught of client comments. Whereas I'm told that it's well known among account handlers that most creatives, when faced with client comments, simply fold up like sofa-beds.

Even the most useless account handler has an advantage when it comes to presenting work—the benefit of being an intermediary. It's more believable when an intermediary pleads a case than when the plaintiff himself does it, because it looks less self-interested. Plus, it's hard for a client to say directly to the person who had an idea: *"I don't like it."* Normally, and quite understandably, they will pretend they like it in the meeting, then call the account team a couple of days later and say: *"Actually...I don't like it."* So you will have wasted your time and theirs.

The time cost of presenting work can be a big factor, depending on how far away the client is based. Even a meeting with a client who is based just a few blocks away always seems to take half a day. Time you could be having ideas in. (Or surfing the internet.)

And the more time you spend with a client, the more you will get to know their business problems. That may sound healthy, but often isn't. You can get bogged down in all their day-to-day concerns, all the internal stakeholders they have to please, and goals and sub-goals they have to meet. You're a creative; you need to sit outside that. You need to have a general understanding of it all, and yet be aloof from it. How else can you give the client a fresh perspective?

BUCKING THE TREND?

In the last few years, the trend around the world has definitely been for creatives to spend more time presenting to clients. Some believe this is a change for the better. Personally, I don't. Instead of spending their time where it's most productive—generating wonderful original ideas—creatives are in meetings presenting to clients. We are doing what account people used to do so brilliantly.

Many creatives are not natural presenters—many are introverts, whereas you'd struggle to find an account handler who isn't at the chattier end of the bell curve. I don't see much benefit in asking the writer to stand up and sell, while the salesperson stays sitting down, and writes notes.

That's why I believe that if you can avoid presenting to clients, you should do so.

However, if your agency has a policy that creatives present the creative work, then how should you go about doing it? The process of presenting to clients breaks down into two phases: "in the room," and "before you go in the room."

BEFORE YOU GO INTO THE ROOM

Before you go into the room, you should be marshaling the best reference you can. But don't show too much. I have seen creatives present five separate pieces of reference for a single press ad, saying *"this one's a reference for the color palette but don't look at the models, they aren't right; for the models you need to look at this other piece of reference, but don't look at the lighting on that one; for the lighting we have this other shot…"* Most confusing. Keep the reference simple; find one or two pieces that say everything you want to say.

Rehearse with the account team what issues may come up. Rehearse your presentation as many times as you need to.

Make sure you know the names of the clients before you go in. People like to be called by their names. Make sure you know who does what, so you don't ask their research manager a question about their TV budget, for example. And make sure you know who the key buyer is. Focus your energy on them, while not excluding the other people in the room.

IN THE ROOM

Once in the room, presenting to the client is much like presenting to the account team. Plenty of preamble is needed. Much of the set-up may be done by the planners and account handlers, but there may be some for you to do too.

For TV projects, you may need to make a mood film—a film made of clips from movies or other ads—which demonstrates your idea. For a print ad, bear in mind that the more finished your concept looks, the more the client will expect their finished ad to look exactly like that. So you're in danger of creating a straitjacket for yourself.

> "I get around this by drawing the concept very roughly, then blowing it up big so it looks more impressive than just a scribble," says Paul Belford, one of the UK's most awarded art directors. "I get the client to buy the concept first; and only then do I show reference material."

Don't treat any of this lightly, thinking that your "real job" is to come up with the ideas. The most successful creatives aren't just the ones who are good at coming up with ideas; they're good at selling them too.

> "When a great showman like Alex Bogusky walks into a room…well, clients can get a little star-struck," says John January, executive creative director of Sullivan Higdon & Sink, Kansas City. "Clients will tell you time again that a strong strategic process is what wins business. But this is a justification. They still love a good show. Would we have it any other way?"

PRESENTATION TIPS

· Keep reference simple
· Rehearse with the account team
· Get your set-up right
· Show your conviction

CONVICTION CONVINCES

"How to sell an advertising idea" could be an entire book in itself, so I'll restrict myself to just one main point: nothing convinces more than conviction.

When a client looks at a concept, they can tell if it's communicating the wrong message, or if the tone is wrong for their brand. But if nothing is wrong with the ad, and they begin to suspect it may be "right," the question becomes "how right." And a huge factor that can sway them here is your *conviction*. You have to tell them this ad is going to be great.

Creatives are often accused of being arrogant, and of "talking up" their own work. Well, you have to. Whether your ad gets made or not may depend on how much *you* believe in it.

Perhaps the UK's most famous poster is "Labour Isn't Working," by Saatchi & Saatchi for the Conservative Party in 1979. Those three words, above a shot of people queuing at an unemployment office, became a significant factor in Margaret Thatcher's first election victory.

However, what is less well known is that when the concept was first presented to Mrs Thatcher, she didn't like it. *"This poster advertises Labour,"* she told Maurice Saatchi. *"On the contrary, Margaret,"* he replied. *"It demolishes them."*

One of the reasons I particularly like this story is that I just love the word "demolishes." But the real lesson here is Maurice Saatchi's conviction.

"Labour Isn't Working" poster by Saatchi & Saatchi

THE TOP TEN OBJECTIONS YOU WILL HEAR AND HOW TO GET AROUND THEM

1 Mrs Thatcher's objection to "Labour Isn't Working" was actually a common one—the accusation of "showing the negative."

In my opinion, there's absolutely nothing wrong with showing the negative. What did Volkswagen's famous *"If only everything was as reliable as a Volkswagen"* campaign show? A negative—*un*reliability. Another example—the amazing viral ad in which a baby shoots out of the womb and flies through the air, ageing from young man, to middle-aged man, to old man, before plunging headlong into a grave just 60 seconds later, thus demonstrating the ultimate negative—that life is short (it's an ad for Xbox, tagline: *"Play more."*)

If someone levels the "showing the negative" accusation at you, try the above examples. However, I've noticed that when people *do* like an ad that shows the negative, they use different language to describe it—they call it a "problem-solution" ad, or say that it's "demonstrating the need for the product." They normally only make the complaint that it's "showing the negative" if there's some other reason they don't like it, which they can't articulate. It's worth trying to find out what that reason is.

2 A frequent objection you may hear about your work is that it's "off-brief;" this normally coming from the account handlers or the planners. Since the brief is a set of guidelines, and it's quite obvious if your work doesn't follow them, this objection is often stated very forcefully, with an assumption that it is terminal. But it needn't be.

To get around this objection, you need to argue that the brief was an excellent battle plan, which was believed to be the best way to achieve the client's objective, but if your work achieves that objective in a different way, then surely it doesn't matter whether it follows the plan. The true goal is to win the war, not to follow the battle orders. In summary, you need to argue that the work you are proposing will create the desired output, even though it may not be based on the agreed input.

3 "Wrong tone" is a tricky objection, one that you are most likely to hear from a creative director, but potentially also the account team and clients. It arises because each brand communicates in its own "tone of voice"— for example, a beer brand and an upmarket Sunday newspaper may both use humor, but the beer may communicate with a populist, laddish type of humor, while the Sunday paper may use a cleverer, witty tone of voice. Do an ad for one in the style of the other, and you'll be told *"it's a great idea, but not right for this client."*

This objection is best anticipated and dealt with in advance, because it's quite difficult to get people to see a joke in an entirely new way when they've heard it once in a certain style.

The truth is that tone is easy to manipulate. For example, I have seen a sexist and vulgar sketch from the *Benny Hill Show* turned into a classy and romantic commercial for a mobile phone network. The creator of this multi-award-winning commercial was clever, and anticipated that a Benny Hill gag could be rejected for being "wrong tone." So he was careful when writing the script that it didn't read like a Benny Hill gag, and he never showed the Benny Hill sketch as a reference.

If you haven't dealt with the "wrong tone" complaint in advance, you can still get around it, but you will need to do a complete rewrite of the script, or redraw of the concept, and provide entirely new reference.

4 The objection that an idea is "too expensive" is one you may hear from clients, TV producers, or account handlers. If you are hearing it from the client, it may mean that they don't actually like the idea that much. (When a client really likes an idea, they somehow always find the money.) However, if it's a genuine budgetary issue, you may be able to get around it, with a little ingenuity.

In the film *Monty Python and the Holy Grail*, one of the most memorable gags is that the knights "gallop" on foot, while clapping coconut halves together to simulate the noise of horses' hooves. But that wasn't the original plan. Before filming began, the budget was cut, and there was no longer enough money for horses.

So if someone tells you there isn't enough money for your project, take a closer look and see if there are any "horses" you can cut. Since simpler is always better, and often funnier, this objection may even improve your idea.

5   The objection that your idea "has been done before" is potentially fatal. You will normally hear this one from your creative director, and he uses it like a person wielding a high-powered assault rifle, fully expecting that it will kill with a single shot. However, with emergency surgery, you may be able to save it.

The reality is that every idea has been done before, in some form or other. And no creative director is really expecting that what you show him will be wholly dissimilar from any piece of communication previously produced on planet Earth. He just wants to see things that *feel* fresh.

You may be able to get around his objection by changing the execution of your idea, so it *appears* radically different to anything that has gone before. Or try removing the most familiar elements of your idea, and placing a bigger emphasis on the less familiar parts. If a story is well known, try looking at what happens before the story, or after it. If an object is over-familiar, try looking at it from a different angle. In advertising, we're often saying something that's been said before. But that needn't matter, if you can find a fresh way of saying it.

6   "Not a big enough idea" is probably one of the more annoying objections you will hear. This can come from anyone, and means one of two things—either that your idea can't be translated into other media, or that it's a "one-off" that isn't "campaignable."

The first of those is easy to get around—you just have to show how your idea does adapt, by coming up with some executions in different media. An idea is an abstract concept that is not dependent on the medium it's expressed in, so if you do have a genuine idea, this should be possible. If it proves difficult, write your idea down purely as a set of words, not an ad. From there, it should be possible to "stretch" it.

7   The objection that an idea doesn't "have legs" is, I think, outdated. The days when campaigns ran for three, five, or ten years seem like a long time ago now. By all means, demonstrate how your idea can work for the first three years. But if someone asks you how your idea is going to develop in years three to five, just tell them they're being unrealistic. The product may not even exist by then.

8   Occasionally, you may hear that an idea is "too big;" in other words, that it implies a whole new positioning for the brand. This annoyingly back-handed compliment can be addressed by incorporating some reference to the brand's existing campaign into your idea.

9   When someone says "I don't get it," there is absolutely no point explaining it to them. The mere fact that you had to explain it will "prove" that the idea is too complicated. View this objection as an opportunity to simplify your idea. Most likely, you'll be improving it.

10   *"They just don't like it…they don't like the color…they think it's too dramatic…too depressing…too funny…"* all these objections and more, you will hear at some point in your career. They are all meaningless. When you hear an objection that sounds more or less random, there is nothing you can do to combat it. Push the person until you find out what their real problem is.

In general, when dealing with an objection, make sure that you treat it as a genuine issue. Never reject a comment out of hand, just because it conflicts with your original vision. After all, what if it's an improvement? Advertising is very much a collaborative process, and over the course of your career you will work with many brilliant planners, creative directors, account handlers, and yes, even clients, all of whom have a legitimate role to play, and all of whom will make your work better, from time to time. And even if you're convinced that an objection is invalid or damaging, don't dismiss it over-harshly or over-swiftly, as the person who made it could become riled, and the objection could become personal.

On the other hand, if you sense that an objection is completely invalid, not strongly held, or just being raised as a protest, then ignore it. It could go away.

There are times when fighting an objection just makes the other person more entrenched in their position.

If you know that your solution is right, then sometimes the smart thing to do is wait. Let them explore other options for a while. When these don't work, they will come back to yours. Many, many good ideas didn't get bought the first time round. Just make sure you have the idea saved on your hard drive. Its time will come.

Finally, bear in mind that obstinacy should be a tactic, not a way of life.

Jamie Barrett, ECD at Goodby Silverstein, San Francisco says that;

"Too many people confuse obstinacy with creative integrity. A good creative person has to be willing to find greatness in what is sometimes an extremely small area. What is the coolest idea you can possibly come up with? What will the client actually buy? Where do those two things intersect? That's the hardest thing for a creative person to learn, and ultimately what separates the best from the rest."

GETTING STUFF READY FOR RESEARCH

One of the most important stages in selling your work is getting it through research.

Creatives generally have one of two feelings about research—they either fear it, or hate it.

There is a myth that "in the old days" nothing was researched. Supposedly, clients had the balls to buy brave work, without stopping to worry what opinion consumers might have of it.

I don't believe this for a minute.

Of course, there *were* brave clients in the past. John Meszaros, a legendary chief marketer at Audi in the UK, famously never used a focus group in his life. When an account man once asked if he wanted to research one of the agency's ideas, Meszaros replied: *"Are you saying my judgement's no good?"*

But there are brave clients today also. Clients who understand that breakthrough work doesn't play well in groups.

However, they're in the minority. Most clients prefer to research ideas before they will approve them. Highly finished visuals will be created to research a print concept. For a TV commercial, they will ask the agency to prepare storyboards, sometimes accompanied by a "narrative" that is either read out to consumers by the researcher, or recorded in advance by a voiceover artist. Sometimes the storyboards are filmed, with added sound effects and camera moves, to create what's called an "animatic."

RESEARCH HORROR STORIES

The way most creatives deal with research…is to complain about it. They explain to the account man in great detail how research groups are an artificial environment, how participants in groups don't tell the truth, how they are easily influenced by the one loudmouth you always get in the bunch, and how some of the world's best-loved campaigns—such as *"Heineken refreshes the parts other beers cannot reach"*—were roundly rejected when put in front of focus groups.

They tell horror stories about how consumers in research groups are asked to move a joystick up and down to indicate how much they are enjoying a commercial. And they laugh about the "cheesy" ads, which they claim are the only ones that do well in research.

Some creatives even go so far as to make humorous films, deriding what happens in research. In the most famous example, which you can find by typing "*1984 focus group*" into YouTube, a group of consumers who have never seen Apple's "1984" are exposed to the storyboards, and complain that it is "*bizarre, creepy, drab, and depressing.*" They then suggest all manner of embarrassing "improvements," such as adding brighter colors, animals, or even having the stormtroopers break into freestyle dance moves.

Anyway, here is an important newsflash: research is not going away.

However right or wrong, good or bad, flawed, embarrassing and wrong-headed the research game may be, it is here to stay.

Therefore, the smart creative learns how to win at it.

HOW TO BEAT THE RESEARCH PROCESS

The first principle to bear in mind, if you want to get your idea through research, is that you need to make it much more obvious than you think you do.

Bill Bernbach once said: "*How do you storyboard a smile?*" He was right. You can't communicate the full emotional impact of a smile on a real human face, in a drawing. Therefore, you are going to have to exaggerate it. When you brief the storyboard company, instruct them to make that smile the biggest, widest, whitest-teeth smile they've ever drawn.

I was once amazed to see an animatic made by a wily team at DDB London, for a Marmite commercial. The script concerned a (male) lifeguard who goes to the aid of a (male) bather and, when administering the kiss-of-life, gets drawn into a full-on snog, because the bather is enraptured by his Marmitey breath. In the script, and indeed in the final commercial, the kiss was handled with subtlety. But in the animatic…a cartoony pair of pouting lips, planting themselves repeatedly on the other guy's lips—backward and forward, at least eight times—accompanied by the cheesiest smooching sound-effect I had ever heard.

I learned a big lesson that day. You may want your ad to be subtle and clever. But your animatic shouldn't be. Your animatic needs to be simple and obvious.

The animatic is not what is going to run. You will not be made to stick to the tone of it—everyone understands that it's basically a cartoon. So cheat. Make the idea clearer than a windowpane in bright sunlight.

Cheat with the narrative as well.

It isn't good writing to have your script say: "*Sally is cross with Jim, because he's stolen her yogurt from the fridge.*" You're supposed to write only what you can shoot. However, for research, you should forget all about good writing. If it helps to say: "*Sally is cross with Jim, because he's clearly enjoying the deliciousness of her yogurt, savoring its fruity taste and obvious health benefits,*" then write it.

A final note about research. The UK's finest-ever creative, John Webster, was a huge fan of it.

He wanted people to like his ads.

He would engage fully with the research process, and chat extensively to the planners and researchers. His idea was to use research for his benefit. He believed that if used in the right way, research could improve his ideas, not destroy them.

For example, when he created the character of the Hofmeister bear for Hofmeister lager, he insisted that the researchers shouldn't ask people whether it made sense for a bear to talk, or endorse this particular brand of lager. Instead, he had them ask questions like "*Which of these outfits do you see the bear wearing?*" and "*What kind of accent should the bear have?*" He presented the bear as a fact, while everything else was negotiable.

During research, the Hofmeister bear duly evolved from John's original conception of a suave James Bond-esque bear in a dinner jacket, to a gruff working-class bear in a baseball jacket.

And if a few people in research groups helped determine what the bear was going to wear, then so what?

John got his bear.

HOW TO DEAL WITH REJECTION

One day, a creative director was asked to do some training for the agency's account handlers. So he had them spend the morning making a model airplane. Then, at lunchtime, he reviewed their work. He took each plane in his hand and crushed it to pieces. *"That,"* he said, *"is what it feels like to be a creative."*

The story probably isn't true, but it does illustrate one of the harder aspects of the creative's job—daily rejection of our work.

WHY REJECTION IS SO PAINFUL FOR CREATIVES

There are several reasons why the rejection we face is so painful.

First of all, it's so frequent. As I mentioned in Chapter 1, you will probably find that at least 99 percent of all the ideas you ever have will be rejected.

It's a brutal kind of rejection too. Many ad ideas contain something of the creator—they might be based on a childhood memory, or a scene from your favorite movie. So the rejection can feel very personal. Creatives often refer to their "babies being killed." A little harsh perhaps, but the analogy to another personal creation has some validity.

> *Few other professions face the brutality of failure we do. As David Droga once put it: "If I were a surgeon, and nine out of ten of my patients died, I would seriously question whether I should be in the industry." But for us, that kind of failure is normal.*

Or compare with the job a builder has—every single brick he lays becomes part of a house. At the end of each day, he has the satisfaction of having built something solid and tangible. But a creative may spend all day working on ideas that get rejected, and at the end of the day have nothing at all to show for his labors.

Sometimes, entire months can be wasted. And it may be through no fault of the team's. Projects can get shelved for all kinds of reasons.

Unfortunately, there is no way around the problem of rejection, only better ways of dealing with it.

VIEWING REJECTION IN A POSITIVE LIGHT

There are some creatives who have an amazing ability to view our 99 percent rejection rate as a positive. The thinking goes something like this: since every time an idea is rejected, an accompanying reason is given, it's possible to view each new rejection as a new piece of information about the brief. Or about the taste of the person issuing the rejection. Your CD was once bitten by an orang-utan and will not countenance any primate-based TV ads? That's a good learning.

According to this theory, each rejection is valuable, and is actually bringing you a step closer to success.

It's also vital you don't see the rejection as a rejection of yourself, however personal the work is to you. Remember that the rejector has no clue of your autobiographical inspiration; they're purely reacting to the piece of paper they see in front of them. And if they reject a route based on a piece of music or an artist who is significant to you, they're not criticizing your taste, they're just saying that your choice isn't right for this brief.

Sometimes it's worth sharing the pain with another team, or a trusted friend. If the friend doesn't think much of your idea, then you realize you haven't lost much anyway. And if the friend thinks it was brilliant, then at least you will get a lot of sympathy.

PRACTICAL STEPS

There are some practical steps you can take to minimize the pain of rejection. Immediately after a negative meeting or review, ensure you have some time alone with your partner to fully curse the account team/ client/creative director. You shouldn't feel bad about doing this. You don't even really mean it. It's just a letting off of steam.

However, after you've comprehensively ridiculed the account team/client/creative director, you must be careful not to turn the gun on yourself. It's tempting to follow a slagging-off session with a sulk. We all like to wallow in sadness sometimes, but in a professional context, it's not helpful. The initial anger that follows the rejection is helpful, I believe, because it releases frustration. But sulking is bad, because you can get sucked into a downward spiral, when what you need to do is move forward.

Sitting there feeling sad because the world doesn't recognize your genius is not going to make you happy. Only getting the world to recognize your genius will. And for that, you need an ad that *does* get bought. So don't sulk. You should rant, clear your head, and then get back to work.

Your first job is to work out how total this rejection is. They've said no to your idea, but did they reject the whole thing, or is there one bit of it you can salvage? Or build on? What new ideas can emerge, like a phoenix from the ashes?

If the rejection *is* total, you can console yourself with the thought that it may not be final. Right now, they've said no to your idea. But you may be able to bring it back later, when the brief still hasn't been cracked, and they're desperate.

And although your idea may not be right for the brief as it stands…the brief can often change. I know of a creative who had a TV ad made fully *seven years* after he first presented the script. When he first wrote the ad, the tone of the idea was wrong for that brand. But over time, the brand's tone evolved and, eventually, his script became right.

So put your rejected work in the bottom drawer.

A good idea never dies. It just sits in limbo, like a lost soul, waiting for the right body.

Jeff Benjamin

INTERACTIVE EXECUTIVE CREATIVE DIRECTOR
CRISPIN PORTER + BOGUSKY, USA

What do you think are the most important qualities an advertising creative needs—above and beyond being good at advertising?
Patience, passion, and persistence.

I've heard that you originally wanted to be a lawyer… was it something you studied at college, and if so does it still help you today?
I debated competitively in college, so the most obvious thing to go into was law. But what I liked about being a lawyer was what I saw on television—being in front of people, being witty, funny, thinking quickly, persuading people, interacting with audiences. In real life that actually has nothing to do with law, and really had more in common with advertising. I think that's why I enjoy my job so much. And that time in college debating helped mold me into the creative I am today.

The main thing young teams want is simply a job. Why do some people get hired relatively quickly and others take longer…or maybe never get hired at all?
When I interview young creatives I look for passion. That's what got me as far as it did. It definitely wasn't my portfolio. Because I realized so late that I wanted to go into advertising, my portfolio was made up of a bunch of brightly colored table tents for musical acts and modern dance groups. To this day I'm baffled as to how I got my first job—which was at a pretty good place. I like to think the passion I had and showed was worth taking a risk for. I think when you're that passionate about something, you figure out how to make up for what you don't have or haven't learned yet.

You have won more than a few awards in your time, including the Interactive Grand Prix at Cannes. Are awards important to a successful career?
I think when you're young they are. As an industry, we create that mentality by rewarding creatives and agencies who have won awards. And when you're young, it's easy to get caught up in it all. But for me, there's no greater reward than seeing something you worked on find its way into the culture. Early in my career, I was at a public library and just coincidentally saw this mom and her young son at a computer near me laughing over something that I had worked on. It's amazing when you can feel like you matter or affect someone. And no lion or pencil can give you that.

It's said that presenting interactive ideas to clients is a little harder than presenting, for example, a poster layout. Is it important for creatives to be good presenters?

It's the most important thing. You could have the greatest idea, but unless you can communicate that idea, it will never see the light of day. Interactive ideas are more challenging because it's often difficult for a client or even a creative director to imagine what you're talking about. Frequently I find that people presenting interactive ideas don't realize what is important about their idea. I would often find myself trying to explain the technology instead of the idea and it would leave people puzzled. When I started talking about the basic concept, the idea, or story first, it was something more people could relate to and get excited about.

It's important to note, though, that while I think presenting interactive work has challenges because it can sometimes require some imagination, it shouldn't be because the idea is complicated. There's a tendency for interactive creatives to complicate their ideas under the belief that the more layers you add on to an idea the better it will be. But all you do is make it more complicated. The best ideas, even interactive ones, have always been simple.

What's the hardest thing about being a creative, and what's the best thing?

For me, it was having a life. Agencies don't really teach life skills. No one is going to tell you when to go home or that you should have some hobbies and a life outside of work. I found myself sort of in a martyr syndrome at the office at all hours and didn't realize all those other things are necessary for a healthy career and help to inspire what happens at the office. I think I went into depression one year when I didn't win some award. That's when I realized there was a problem.

For me, being an inventor is the best part. Probably most interactive creatives share that love. I think I was maybe a scientist in another life because I can't help but want to make things that don't exist. Solve problems that don't have solutions. Be a pioneer. And then work with other people as a team to solve those things.

Do you think any creative can work well in any medium, or are there some teams who will always be better at print, or interactive, or whatever?

More and more, creatives are becoming multi-dimensional. Especially young ones. And really, at this point, if you're a young creative, you have to be good at every medium if you want a job. If you're someone who's been in the industry for a while now, I think that time where you could hide behind nice print and TV has come to an end. And it's because as an industry, we've realized that truly great ideas, the big ideas, are bigger than any one medium. And many times, invent mediums of their own.

You made a successful move from Goodby Silverstein to CP&B —when is the right time for a creative to move agencies?

The best time to make a move is when you feel like you're running toward something great, and not running away from something bad. Too many times, creatives make ill-fated moves because they're trying to get away from what they think is a bad situation. Whether they feel like they're being held back or aren't making enough money or hate the smell of their partner. You know you're making a great decision when you can't wait to start somewhere because of the amazing opportunity that awaits.

To be creative do you have to "live creative"?

I go through life with the filter of interactive. I buy movies and music online. I'm a part of all the social networks; I twitter, I play video games even though I have no co-ordination, I try to experience everything you can possibly experience or do in the digital world. And as I'm experiencing those things and the everyday things that go on in my life—in the back of my mind, I'm thinking about what sort of creative idea that might inspire. If I have a problem or wish something existed that doesn't, I wonder if other people might have that problem too, and whether a client we have could bring a solution to the world. It's important to live in the mediums we work in because that's the only way we'll know if we're creating the right solutions for our clients.

A final word of advice for young creatives?

Remember to have fun and enjoy your career. We work in an industry that nurtures unrealistic dreams like wanting to be the youngest art director, then a creative director, making the most money, winning the most awards. And unfortunately, when you get caught up in that kind of thinking, you're left unfulfilled and disappointed. It's like going to an amazing restaurant and basically inhaling all the food. Eating so fast that you never enjoy the meal, but focus on getting the meal into your stomach before anyone else at the table does. Enjoy every moment of your career, learn everything you can, and remember that coming up with great ideas, making things, seeing people play with the stuff that you make—all of that is what you'll remember in your career. And what you might be remembered for. Not how much you make, when you got a promotion, or that time you were on stage winning an award.

CHAPTER 6
HOW TO GET THE BEST OUT OF THE PEOPLE YOU WORK WITH

Bill Green, the US art director and author of the popular ad blog _Make the Logo Bigger_, claims that when he was a student, a senior creative told him: _"Be nice until you get in, then you can be an asshole."_

Amusing as that quote is, I'd say there's _never_ a reason to be rude to anybody, and plenty of reasons to be civil.

Some creatives find this hard—perhaps because our job is primarily about ideas, not people; we are constantly hunting something down in our minds, and being civil takes effort, and means you have to snap out of your train of thought.

But it's worth it.

First of all, it won't help your career if you get a reputation for being rude. And it _will_ help if you have a reputation for being friendly and likeable. So even if you're not naturally warm and cuddly, it really is worthwhile to at least be polite and good-tempered.

Quite simply, you'll find people are more likely to help you if you're nice to them.

Always bearing in mind...you don't want to be so gentle that you fade into the background.

This may be more of an issue in some countries than others. Simon Welsh, executive creative director at BBDO Guerrero in the Philippines, points out that it's part of most Asian cultures to respect one's elders, much more so than in the West;

"As a result, many young creatives are too shy and respectful to give their point of view. Those with the self-confidence to stand up for their ideas (as long as they do so without calling their boss an ignorant tosser) can go far."

When I was starting out, every creative department had several PAs who typed the creatives' scripts and kept track of their whereabouts.

Nowadays, all creatives can type and have mobiles, so the role of departmental PA has disappeared. But the executive PA, who "looks after" a creative director, remains.

It may be argued that a personal assistant is more of a luxury than an essential. For sure, part of the job involves booking restaurants, fetching coffee, and buying flowers for the CD's wife and mistress. And yet... even these trivial duties may be invaluable. A creative director's time is costly; it makes sense for an agency to get the most out of it. For example, it probably works out ten or 20 times cheaper for the agency to send a PA to buy his sandwich than for the CD to go out and buy his own.

But the executive PA plays another, truly crucial role—managing the "Tetris" that is the CD's diary. Most creative directors have far more people wanting to see them than there is time available, which means their diaries are completely overloaded. _"I quickly saw that even 'bottom scratching: 5 mins' needed to be scheduled"_: the words of one ex-PA.

Diary-handling means that the PA wields a great deal of power—as the CD's gatekeeper. Since everyone who wants to see the CD says it's urgent, it's up to the PA to decide which cases really are urgent, which can wait, and which just don't need to happen at all.

So make sure you get on with her. If a CD's PA likes you, she's more likely to find time in his diary for you, more quickly. More time with the CD means better feedback, less time wasted, and more opportunities for you.

A minority of PAs, it's true, are rude. Some of them think that just because they are near to the top person, they have the right to behave as if they are at the top too. A copywriter with 12 years' experience in the industry can understandably get annoyed when a 22-year-old, who knows nothing whatsoever about advertising, treats him like dirt.

They believe they can get away with acting like gods because whatever they do, you'll still have to be nice to them. And they're correct. Unfortunately, however arrogant or difficult a PA may be, you cannot be snappy, as this will get reported back to the boss, and it is _you_ who will end up with the reputation of being arrogant or difficult.

You *have* to get on with this person. And it isn't actually that hard. In some agencies, the PA may be a wannabe creative, so you will naturally have lots in common, and you may even be able to help each other out. In other agencies, the PA may be a "professional PA," who may be of a different gender to you, a different educational background, and have different goals. Well, so what. You get on with this person the same way you get on with anyone else in life—find out what you *do* have in common, and talk about that.

(As an added incentive, bear in mind that PAs are often at the center of the agency's social life, have all the best gossip, and always have the CD's credit card when it needs to be placed behind a bar.)

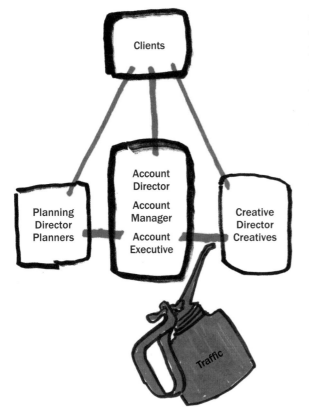

HOW TO GET THE BEST OUT OF TRAFFIC

Traffic (also known as progress or project management —the department goes by different names in different agencies) does a job similar to that of air traffic control at an airport; managing the flow of work through the agency, and bringing each project safely home.

When a client decides they need to advertise, the planner and account team will write a brief for what the advertising should say and what it's expected to achieve.

They will also let the traffic department know, and while the brief is still being prepared, the traffic department, along with the account team and creative director, discuss how to resource it—whether it's a relatively simple brief that can go to a single junior team, or whether it's a big opportunity (or a big problem) that they want a more senior team to tackle, or several teams, and whether there are any creatives whose skills or interests make them particularly suitable for this brief.

For example, if one of the agency's clients is sponsoring the FIFA World Cup, that brief is best placed with a team who like soccer. If the client is sponsoring the National Ballet, that brief may go to a different team.

Once the brief has been assigned, the traffic person organizes all the meetings that need to happen—the briefing session for the planner to brief the creatives, any research trips or brainstorms that may be taking place, creative reviews in which the creatives will present their work to the creative director, and the meeting to present the work to the client.

The traffic person monitors the process closely— ready to move meetings back if it looks like the project will need more time, or add more teams if the assigned ones don't crack the brief.

Once the client has approved the work, the traffic person supervises its production. Most agencies have specialist TV producers who look after TV and radio production, and perhaps digital producers who look after online work. But it's normally the traffic person who supervises print work, which may include sourcing and negotiating with photographers, or buying stock shots (though some agencies have a separate department called art buying, which takes care of that).

Then once the job is completed, the traffic person puts a big line through it on their worksheet. They love organizing—their idea of an hour well spent is an hour sorting out their to-do list.

Bear in mind that some traffic people are professional project managers and aren't necessarily interested in advertising. As far as they're concerned, they could be shepherding boxes of machine tools through the system. That's fine. Their efficiency and problem-solving skills can add a lot to the process, even if they wouldn't know the difference between Frank Budgen and Franklin Gothic. Others *do* have a strong interest in advertising, or design. They may have a wealth of information they can pass on about the sort of work the client normally buys, or which photographers to use for your project.

In general, traffic are rarely the best-paid, highest-educated, or most ad-literate people in the building, but they do play a crucial role. Like the oil that lubricates an engine, you may not think they're as significant as the more glamorous parts like the pistons or the spark plugs, but you would certainly notice if they disappeared. The whole system would grind to a halt.

In my first year in advertising, I once asked a senior creative—*"Who's it better to be really in with—the account handlers or the planners?"*

His reply was *"Traffic."*

Of course you should make friends with everybody. But there are good reasons to make a special effort with traffic.

REASONS TO MAKE A SPECIAL EFFORT WITH TRAFFIC

First of all, they know when the good briefs are coming up. And if they like you, they might even give you one. Nowadays, many agencies put all briefs that are currently "in the system" up on their intranet, so there's greater transparency than there used to be, and perhaps less need to sneak around, or buy drinks for a traffic person, to find out what's going on. But it's still worth consulting traffic if you're interested in a brief, because they'll have more knowledge than you could glean from the mere listing—like whether it's a real opportunity or not.

Traffic may also know which juicy brief a senior team are struggling on; get ready to jump in.

If you like gossip (and let's face it, you do) the traffic department—because they get around the building so much—can tell you who is about to be fired, who is sleeping with whom, and other such tidbits.

They can also, if you ask them nicely, give you more of the most precious commodity of all. Time. Always communicate openly and honestly with your traffic person. If you are struggling with a brief, there's a natural tendency to lie, and pretend that everything's fine, because it's embarrassing to admit to being in difficulties. However, you'll be much better off telling the truth. Sure, you should embellish a little—explain how you've been soooooooo busy on other projects, and how you lost a couple of days when the planner had to go away to clarify that one crucial detail...no one wants to look bad, after all. But if you admit when you're in trouble, and the traffic person has sympathy for you, they may be able to buy you a little more time, by putting back a deadline somewhere else in the process.

The head of traffic is especially important, because that person is heavily involved in brief allocation. If you can give the head of traffic the impression that you are a bright, lively, friendly, and hard-working team, then so much the better—they will put you up for good briefs.

Upset them, and you'll find yourself doing briefs for tray-mats, where your work will be a surface onto which people squirt the little sachets of ketchup in McDonald's. So, make friends with traffic. It will do you good to talk to someone who isn't called Tarquin or Julian for a change.

HOW TO GET THE BEST OUT OF DIRECTORS

There's a lot of mystique around directors.

Who flies a runner from Iceland to Soho to bring back a certain coffee bean for him? Who's shagging whom, who can't get work any more, who's getting 50 scripts a week, who's just moved to a new production company for a signing-on fee of $2 million? Most of it's hearsay. But we still love hearing it all.

Creatives obsess about directors. Maybe that's because you can't choose your account team, your client, or your CD...but you do get to choose your director. And the director has a bigger influence than anyone else on the final film.

The director's job is to take your script and turn it into a finished commercial. He will have an overall vision for how he wants the ad to look and feel, and over the course of the production, he will make hundreds of decisions that shape the commercial, including which actors to cast, which locations to shoot in, the set, how the commercial should be edited, and what music (if any) should accompany it.

Of course, you are there too, and you have a big say as well. He has to get his major decisions (e.g. casting) approved by you, and in turn you get these approved by your client. But he will make many more decisions than you do. For example, he may show you two or three locations he has in mind for the commercial, but he himself may have looked at hundreds. And in choosing the location manager, in a sense he's already chosen the kind of locations he will be choosing from, as certain location managers might be known for finding quirky-looking settings, or edgy ones, etc.

The director is a lot more than just someone behind the camera in a waterproof jacket saying "action." His taste and aesthetic will run through every frame of your commercial, like the DNA in every cell of a body.

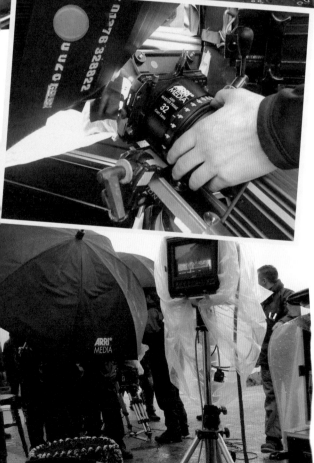

That's why the most important skill for a creative in terms of "getting the best from" directors is simply picking the right one in the first place.

The TV department keep the showreels of hundreds of directors, and they will help you pick out some who might be suitable. When looking at reels, you are basically looking for a director who is good at making the kind of ad you want to make. If it's a dialogue-driven ad, find a director who is great at doing dialogue. If you're looking to create an extremely beautiful piece of film, find a director with a beautiful reel.

Easy, right? Yes. In fact, it's too easy. I hate it when creatives tell me they want an ad to be "beautiful." That's such a vague and generic term. There are so many different kinds of beauty—there's the plastic beauty of a catwalk model, the rugged beauty of the coast of Cornwall, the ethereal beauty of the Northern Lights, the sinister beauty of an over-ripe pomegranate, the innocent beauty of a new-born foal…. There are endless sub-categories in every genre of commercial. Think how many different types of humor there are, or how many different types of cool. You'll only find exactly the right director if you define exactly what you're looking for.

Then be realistic about who you ask the TV department to contact. Martin Scorsese won't do a tabletop ad. Don't waste your time thinking, *"But he's never done one of those, it might be interesting for him."* It won't.

In your shortlist of directors, always have a banker and a wild card.

The script you send to directors shouldn't necessarily be the same as the one you send to the client. Who says it has to be? Write a special version of the script that is designed to hook a director. Leave out the lengthy product-description sequence that you put in for the client, and focus on the emotional and visual appeal of the idea. Sometimes a one-line script is all you need. For example, a director may be more attracted to a script that reads *"We drop millions of colored balls down a street in San Francisco"*—a script that allows him to visualize the scene in his mind—rather than a two-page lyrical description you have realized from your own imagination… and thus left him no room to use his.

When meeting directors, you need to decide *"Can I work with them? Do I like them?"* Over the years I've noticed that it doesn't really matter if you and the director have wildly divergent personalities. As long as you have the same vision for the ad, you'll probably get on well. But never work with jerks, however talented. It's just not worth it. If you do fight a lot, then a) you probably picked the wrong director and b) you probably won't end up with a good ad.

DEALING WITH TENSION

There is often tension between the director and creatives. And usually it comes from the creatives being fearful. A script—like a mathematical formula or an architect's plan—is perfect, in the way that no finished artefact can be.

> *When you hand your script to a director, he will turn your perfect Euclidean geometry into rough-hewn reality. Of course, the hope is he will make it better than the blueprint. But the fear that he will cock it up is considerable.*

I remember one shoot of mine where the director was so hyped-up—to avoid libel implications we might say he'd had a cup of extra-strong coffee before walking on set (it was definitely *something* of Colombian origin)—that he was giving each actor a ten-minute monologue of instructions for a single line of dialogue then calling *"Cut"* before they'd finished saying it, and then launching into another long stream of verbal diarrhea. We literally filmed less than two minutes, the whole morning.

Not much you can do when the unexpected happens. But you can at least minimize uncertainty by beating out all the questions that are on your mind before shooting starts, so you're never sitting there on set wondering *"What the hell are they doing now?"*

The most tense part of the job is often the actual shoot. A lot of money is being spent in a short space of time, so people are stressed. And there's never enough time for all the filming you want to squeeze in. That adds to the stress.

For these and other reasons, film sets can be intimidating for young creatives. But remember, it's your ad. And though the director has ultimate power on set, with perhaps 50 people jumping to their command, if the creative says *"Can we try it this other way...?"*, then they have to listen. You feel strange, and guilty, as if you're giving orders to an emperor, but sometimes it has to be done.

The question of "when to intervene" is a tricky one. My approach is that I always give the director space and let them get on and do the shot they want to do. Then if I don't like it, I'll explain why, and ask if they can try it a different way, either as well as or instead of. But let them do it their way first. If you're too controlling, and don't give them the chance to do what they want to do, then why did you hire them? There's also a risk they can become demoralized, and just start to go through the motions.

TIPS FOR WORKING WITH A DIRECTOR

1 Respect a director's way of working. You want to get out of them whatever they can give. So for example if they want their space, and prefer comments to be filtered through a producer, then do that.

2 Don't tell the actors what to do—that's what the director is being paid a lot of money to do. And actors like to hear one voice.

3 During the process of making a commercial, there is no one single way to deal with directors, because every director is different. But there will always be some way that gets a result. Sometimes it's putting your arm around someone; sometimes it's giving them a kick up the backside.

4 Creatives also need to shield their director, to some extent. Especially when it comes to the edit, the post-production, and everything that goes into finishing up a commercial. That's when the account team and client can be at their most meddlesome. Be the champion of your own idea, and don't let the forces of darkness water it down.

HOW TO GET THE BEST OUT OF ACCOUNT HANDLERS

The account handler's basic job is to advise the client on how to move their brand forward, and marshal the agency's resources to deliver that.

They are sometimes called account supervisors, although as well as supervising the account, they are also supervising everyone else in the agency.

They are involved at every stage of the process—discussing with the client what his communications requirements are, liaising with the planners to create a brief, liaising with the creatives as they create work to that brief, leading the selling-in of this work to the client, and then supervising the production and evaluation of the advertising. Along the way, it's their job to solve any problems that arise.

My general advice—you have a much better chance of getting good work made if you work in partnership with account handlers, not in opposition to them.

Never shout at them, or throw laptops out of the window. Or plants. Or chairs.

Some creatives believe there's a creeping blandness about the business that is dulling the creative edge... that the industry *needs* a bit of standing-on-the-window-ledge aggression from all parties, or you end up with compromised work.

But personally, I don't believe that co-operation necessarily leads to compromise. I believe you're actually more likely to get your way if you respect people, listen to them, and work *with* them to explain why your vision is the best way forward. It's less stressful too.

At the briefing stage, don't waste time slagging off the client or the brief. Focus on what the opportunity is, not the problems. And don't be sullen. Ask the questions that will tease out all the vital information the account team knows, which doesn't appear on the brief. For example, what type of work does this client like? What are they expecting for this brief? Do they have any quirks or peculiarities? These questions can yield a string of useful facts, like *"Oh, Phil hates commercials with celebrities. Doesn't think they work. But he loves animation, and...yeah—anything with dogs is a dead cert."* Now that you know to start with an animated puppy, you have saved yourself a lot of time.

Campaign, the British advertising trade magazine, once asked various industry figures: *"What makes a good suit?"*

The list of qualities they came up with included: patience, diplomacy, negotiation skills, ability to get bills paid on time, breadth of experience, eclectic, ability to do strategy and channel planning, helping stimulate good creative work, make things happen, drive change, clever, fun to be around, sociable, likeable, rigorous, relentless, fearless, immune to pressure, unfazed by complexity, clear vision, truth-telling, respect confidences, sense of humor, keep things in perspective, don't try to take credit, no whinging, create, lead, manage, make it happen, be on top of everything, be ruthless, respect authority, know when you can flout convention, recognize the primacy of the idea, have a view on advertising, know everything possible about the client's brand.

How can we expect our account handlers to have all these qualities? No one does. So, let's not be too hard on them.

It's a good trick to make the account team write ads to their brief before they leave your office—sometimes called "Account Man Ads." For example, the Account Man Ad to Sony's "Color Like No Other" brief—the brief that led to "Balls" and "Paint"—might have been *"We open on a rainbow, but instead of the usual seven bands of color, it has thousands."* Not a particularly interesting idea. But it demonstrates that the brief is actually possible to answer, and tells you what the account team thinks the answer may look like.

When you have your idea, explain it as fully as you can to the account team. Talk them through the highlights of your creative journey—they will understand it a lot better if they know how you got to it.

Explain and re-explain "what the idea is."

Make sure they understand which parts of your route are fundamental, and which are the executional details they can sacrifice if the client objects. The account team will probe your idea for weaknesses. This can be frustrating for creatives, as it sounds like they're criticizing your work, but they're actually role-playing how the conversation with the client might go. Play along. They might just sell your concept first time around if you prime them with a few answers to the "why" questions.

And when it comes to the production process, the best thing you can do is keep the account handler in the loop. It's tempting not to tell them things, on the grounds that they might object, and that it takes up time talking them through it. But the more they know, the more they can manage the clients' expectations.

Account handlers do an enormous amount of client hand-holding that is kept far, far away from the creatives. If we only knew half the sh*t they had to do... we would probably feel a lot more grateful toward them.

But, sadly, since the beginning of advertising, there has been tension between creatives and account handlers. *"Our account handlers don't know what they're doing"* or *"This agency is run by the suits"* are perhaps the most common complaints you will hear from creatives in after-hours pub chats.

The solution many creatives seem to have in mind to the "problem" of account handlers is for account handlers to be removed from the process, or at least made totally subservient to the creative department.

I remember one departmental meeting we had at DDB London. The usual festival of complaints about account handlers was interrupted by Larry Barker, the executive creative director. *"Know one thing,"* he said. *"Account handlers are not going away."*

He was right. Account handlers have always been there; and always will.*

The smart thing is to learn to work *with* them. Let's look at the three main causes of all the tension between us and them: they have different priorities to us, a different way of working, and different personalities too.

An account handler friend once told me the story of when a random goat was brought onto the set of a yogurt commercial. The director and creatives wanted to shoot a scene with this goat (for reasons that, alas, are no longer recalled), but since the script hadn't mentioned a goat, and no goat had been discussed in the pre-production meetings, the client freaked out. The account handler had no clue what was going on, so it was the creatives who had to spend the next hour calming the client down and explaining what they planned to do. They did get to shoot their goat in the end, but an hour of valuable time had been lost, and they failed to get the "goat performance" that they wanted. If the creatives had shared the idea during the pre-production stage, there wouldn't have been a problem.

*There are one or two agencies that do not have account handlers—the most notable example is Mother. However, as perhaps 99 percent of you will be working in agencies that do have account handlers, I won't go into detail here about Mother's system. All I will say is that if you go to Mother excited about the prospect of there being no account handlers...be careful what you wish for. It's true there are no account handlers at Mother, but there is account handling—and it's the creatives who have to do it. Some creatives love that, some hate it.

DIFFERENT PRIORITIES

The tension over priorities is that creatives feel account handlers don't care about the quality of the work, only about keeping their client happy.

And, in fact, this complaint is quite accurate.

The main priority of an account handler is not to produce great creative work.

But nor should it be. That's your job. His main job is to keep the client happy. Sometimes that will involve producing great creative work, but only if that is what the client wants.

The different departments of an agency work together like the different parts of a car. The engine produces power; the steering wheel controls direction of travel; the oil lubricates the system. Each element has a totally different function, and each only cares about their own job...and yet that's the best way to make a car go smoothly.

Does the engine complain *"that bloody steering wheel doesn't give a toss about power generation"*? No. So neither should you complain that account handlers don't care about great work.

DIFFERENT WAYS OF WORKING

When an account man walks into your office and you're staring out the window, he'll make a sarcastic comment like *"Hard at work, I see."*

This is because account handlers don't have to think of ideas; their job is talking to people and persuading them to do things. He feels much more comfortable when he comes into your office and sees you're on the phone, or typing on your computer, because that's what he spends *his* day doing.

He doesn't realize that when you're on the phone you are probably talking to friends, and when you're typing on the computer you are probably forwarding a funny YouTube film to one of your mates. And it's only when you are staring into space that you are actually doing your job—trying to think of ideas.

The biggest mystery for account handlers is why the creative floor, supposedly the heartbeat of the agency, has "no buzz." They joke that the atmosphere is *"like a library"* rather than anywhere creative. What they don't realize is that to think of an idea, you need peace and quiet.

If they make sarcastic comments about how you do your job, just ignore them.

DIFFERENT PERSONALITIES

Just as our jobs are different to theirs, the same goes for personalities. They look like us, and they talk like us, but they are not like us. Account handlers are a different species entirely.

For example, an old colleague of my wife's (they're both suits) once came to our house for lunch. They talked about the clients they both knew; people they had both worked with; people who had moved, been fired, promoted; creative directors they had worked with; they discussed who was easy to talk to, who was difficult to deal with, who was going through a divorce...

After they'd been talking for about an hour, I suddenly realized that neither of them had mentioned a single advert.

All they had talked about was people.

When two creatives meet up for a chat, of course we talk about people as well—who's up, who's down, who's round the twist. But we will also talk a lot about advertisements. We will ask the other what they think about the latest Nike work, or Sony work, or whatever. We will talk about ideas we have had, campaigns we are working on, ads that didn't get bought.

Our currency is advertising. Theirs is people. "Account handler" is probably the wrong term. They are really "people handlers."

I sometimes think creatives are experts in *mass* communication—TV ads that aim at millions of people—while account handlers are experts in *personal* communication—meetings where they aim to influence the behavior of just one or two key people (i.e. clients).

Of course, they choose to exercise those skills in the world of advertising, and many of them are fascinated by adverts.

But the main reason they like working in advertising is the people. Bizarrely enough, that means you! Account handlers *like* working with creative people. Yes, we are frustrating and mysterious to them a lot of the time. But they enjoy the challenge. They feel it's less boring than working in a bank or a law firm. And when it comes to working with clients, they enjoy the challenge of trying to understand that person's needs, and persuading them that the agency has met their needs.

So, that is the most important thing to understand about our friends, the suits. They are not, as you are, focused on creating great advertising. They are focused on people, what those people want, and how to influence them.

Because dealing effectively with account handlers is so vital to your success in this business, I think it's worth hearing an account handler's point of view on the subject; the more you understand them, the better.

First, here is an excellent summary from Neil Christie, managing director of Wieden & Kennedy, London, on what he recommends creatives should do to get the best out of suits;

"Give them public recognition for their contribution when it's due. Say thank you. Ask their opinion. Ask if they have any ideas about how the brief should be addressed. Ask questions about the brief that show you've thought about it—especially about the business issues behind the brief. Share ideas with them. Explain why you think a piece of work is right, especially when it's "off brief." Inspire them to feel as passionately about the work as you do. If you make them feel that you value and respect them; that you're working together as a team, then they will move mountains for you."

And now here's an interview with a senior account handler at a Top Ten London ad agency, who promised to tell it like it really is...on condition of anonymity.

You guys are supposed to be the "make it happen" people...so how come you behave more like the "No" department?

I can understand that it may feel that way to creatives. It's your job to come up with ideas and, inevitably, not every single one is going to be right for that piece of business at that time, so we do have to say no quite a lot.

Why can't you just take the idea to the client and let the client be the judge?

That wouldn't be doing our job. We're not just there to jump up and down clapping our hands like seals when you show us the work, you know. In reality, the client briefs us on what they want, and they expect us to get it for them. They don't want us to bring them things they don't want. If we did that, we would quite soon have no clients. However, we do work for the agency—the agency pays our salary, not the clients—so we're always trying to sell the best possible work, which they will buy.

Why do clients so often ask for "more than one route"?

They don't like to be painted into a corner. And they want the best chance possible of seeing work that is right. The fact is that what we do isn't a science. There is always more than one answer. One may be more right than another, but there are always different ways to go. It's a game of subjective judgements and the clients like to be able to participate in that judging too.

Do you treat all creatives the same?

Probably not. After all, no one treats everyone the same way. There are people you like more than others and your attitude and actions towards them will vary accordingly. Friendliness and an appearance that you're listening and being reasonable goes a long way to getting an account team on your side.

HOW TO GET THE BEST OUT OF PLANNERS

Since the dawn of advertising, there has been tension between creatives and planners. Actually, that's not true. At the dawn of advertising, there weren't any planners.

And that is the source of the tension. Some creatives simply feel that planners are unnecessary.

After all, advertising was conducted perfectly satisfactorily before planning was invented (the great DDB Volkswagen ads of the 1960s, for example, were created without a planner in sight).

But good planning adds a lot to the process.

Jeff Goodby, CD and co-chairman, Goodby Silverstein & Partners, told _ihaveanidea.org_:

"If you've ever gone fishing and had a really good guide, you know what the relationship between creatives and planners should be. The planner should know the river and what flies will work at what time of day. The creative people still have to make the cast and land the fish."

Planning was invented (in about 1968) in order to provide three things: greater consumer insight; better strategies; and a focus on effectiveness.

The planner is sometimes called "the voice of the consumer" and, within an agency, the planner will know more than anyone else about the target market for a product. He will have researched it, using reams of data on purchasing patterns, and also spent time with groups of consumers.

Planners are also concerned with "effectiveness," and planners spend a great deal of time attempting to measure the effectiveness of an agency's campaigns, to understand what's working and what isn't working, and how to improve it.

But the planner's main job is to determine the "strategy" for the creative work, a.k.a. "what to say."

This can come as a shock to young creatives. A lot of the feedback you get on your portfolio when you're looking for a job is about your strategies—whether they're original, exciting, or neither. And yet as soon as you get a job, you're no longer responsible for strategy, because the planner is. Odd.

Nevertheless, the fact that most creatives have an excellent understanding of strategy doesn't mean you ought to ignore whatever brief the planner gives you, and write your own. Remember, the brief has been signed off by your creative director, by the head of planning, the senior account handlers on the business...not to mention the client. Some of these people may be keener on the brief than others, but they've all approved it. Even if the strategy you come up with is better than the one on the brief, it may take days to go around all these stakeholders and explain the new direction to them.

For all these reasons, if you ignore the brief, you are much less likely to get your work sold. You may feel that the brief is restrictive, and is preventing you from coming up with a brilliant idea. On the other hand, true brilliance entails coming up with an idea that is both wonderfully creative _and_ on brief.

Having said all that...what if you absolutely hate the brief? First of all, don't say it's rubbish and you can't work with it. Or say _"uh huh"_ and then badmouth the planner once they're out the door, and write to whatever you think the brief should be. Try taking the approach you're supposed to take with your doctor: apparently, after they've made their diagnosis, you should ask _"What else could it be?"_ This forces them to stop and consider other hypotheses.

If the brief is just not working for you, go ahead and talk about it. It's not like it's carved in stone or anything. Though it may have been signed in blood by 100 international marketing directors, in which case it will be tough to get changed. But many briefs are more flexible.

"Talk things out early," recommends David Hackworthy, planning partner at The Red Brick Road in London. "Too many creatives are mute at formal briefing stage."

In any case, good planners don't just brief a creative team and then disappear. Like a good waiter, they will leave you to chew things over for a while, then come back and ask if everything is OK.

One of the best planners I've worked with used to come into our office every single day when we had one of his briefs. He would just sit with us and throw ideas around. He didn't mind if we hated them. Every day he came in with a new random thought, a provocation, or a website he thought might be relevant. He was just always there...up in my grille...even though he was also the agency's head of planning and had numerous other calls on his time. Like all the best planners, he saw his main job as being to *stimulate great work*.

Ultimately, a really good planner doesn't care about the brief. They know the brief is nothing more than a roadmap. If you deliver the car to the right destination, and take a more exciting route than the map was suggesting, they'll be delighted. And when they present your work to the client, they'll find a way to retro-fit the brief to your work.

Creatives are often bursting with a Larry David-esque exasperation about planning. Like most planners, Russell Davies, former head of strategy at Wieden & Kennedy in London, doesn't feel any animosity toward creatives, but he's certainly aware of it coming his way.

Russell theorizes: *"Creatives suffer so much rejection on a daily basis that they need to take it out on someone and that someone tends to be planners."* Neat argument.

As the relationship between creatives and planners is so important, I asked a few experienced planners for some advice of their own.

Russell Davies's tip for getting the best out of planners is... *"Lots of creatives see planners as a necessary evil, and most of the rest see them as an unnecessary evil. So if you're one of the small percentage of creatives who treat them as helpful and interesting colleagues, they will be so pathetically grateful that they'll do all sorts of helpful and interesting things for you."*

"Look up and smile when they enter the room," adds Russell. *"Don't just continue to scowl at your computer until they've sat down and coughed nervously for ten minutes."*

"Demand pictures on the creative brief. Honestly, I can't believe there are still creative briefs without pictures of the people you're supposed to be talking to and the thing you're supposed to be advertising. Pictures help. Refuse to do anything until they've given you pictures."

"Ask them to bring you inspiration and ideas, not just instructions," he goes on. *"The brief should outline the task; the planner should help you solve it. Again, if you ask for thoughts, ideas, inspiration, and then actually listen to what they bring you, you will get tons and tons of interesting and useful stuff. Obviously a large percentage of it will be rubbish, but then a large percentage of your ideas will be rubbish, that's the nature of things. But if you listen, and let them talk, you'll find some unexpected nuggets in there. Things you wouldn't have thought of on your own."*

"Get them to help you sell it. A decent planner is great at crafting an argument for a piece of creative work. Maybe better than you. They may not have been able to come up with it, but they might have more insight about why it's great. Get them to help you put those arguments together, both inside the agency and with the client. They may have a better idea of what the client wants to hear. It's worth running through those conversations with your planner."

*"But, basically, don't be an ar*e. Agency life tends to push people into all sorts of weird status/hierarchy behavior. Most of it is unhelpful. You'll get the most out of your planner if you forget all that stuff and just be nice."*

Sarah Watson, head of planning at DDB in London, says: "*My tip to creatives for getting the best out of planners is...to talk to them. It's all about the conversations. Planners have stuff in their heads that can help you. But it is only when you get talking that you come across the bits that will really unlock things for you and the way you think. Planners are a resource laid on for your benefit—don't forget it, don't waste it, and make sure you use it.*"

Richard Huntington, director of strategy for Saatchi & Saatchi in the UK, advises: "*You should demand the world of the planners you work with. Really powerful strategic ideas and briefs. At their best, a good planner is going to make sure you can't help but produce the best work of your careers. They will do this by placing you from the very start in a territory that no other creative has visited for that brand. This is the reason you will come to depend on them and love them, not because they pop down the pub with you on a Friday lunchtime.*"

However, he goes on to say: "*Always remember, the reason the planner is committed to creating a better beginning for you is not to improve your reel but to make more effective work. And that's where the rub comes. A planner's obligation to make the work work will sometimes see you in healthy tension with them.*"

Elisa Edmonds, a senior planner at Ogilvy in New Zealand, advises that "*a few positive words can bring the best out in your planner.*"

"*We are frequently insecure,*" says Elisa. "*We really, really care—we want it to be great, not just good. We get nervous that our work will be savaged when it's first presented. Any of that sound familiar? If so, you'll know exactly how you like to be treated and know how people who get the best out of you, get the best from you.*"

"*Ask the planner what they looked at for inspiration when writing the brief. This might open up fresh areas for you, and provide good stuff to mull over/discuss together.*"

"*Be interested in what people said in research. Or what they didn't (it's the dog that doesn't bark in the night that can be most interesting).*"

HOW TO WORK WELL WITH CREATIVE DIRECTORS

The main job of the creative director is deciding what work the agency presents to the client.

Smaller agencies have a single creative director who is in charge of every account. Larger agencies will have several CDs, each looking after one or more clients, and above them an executive creative director, who in addition to his account responsibilities does the hiring and firing. Some CDs also write ads, some don't.

As a creative, you mostly see the creative director in so-called creative reviews, during which he looks over the work you have done, and either approves it or suggests changes. But that is only one-quarter of his actual job. His other responsibilities include: finalizing the initial brief with the planner; talking the account team through your work; presenting your work to the client; and having endless meetings with the client about their brand guidelines, tone of voice, and the work in general. That's in addition to meetings with the agency's management about the work, and defining the overall creative vision for that account.

So that's the first thing to bear in mind about creative directors—they are busy. Thus the best way to have a good relationship with your creative director is to crack his briefs quickly and cleanly. In general, creative directors most prize the teams who come up with lots of good ideas...and who don't need much hand-holding.

> "*You should know that most creative directors don't assess you simply by how creative you are,*" is how David Lubars, ECD of BBDO New York, puts it. "*We also consider how deep, how fast, and how willing to return to the well you are. And how much of a pain you are not.*"

Of course, your CD won't expect you to crack every brief first time. And even the simplest job will involve some to-ing and fro-ing. They say it takes two to tango, but with the number of people involved in making an advert, we could do the conga.

Everything takes time, and everything takes meetings. Try to make those meetings painless for him. Yes, ask questions. Yes, ask for guidance—that's what he's there for. But don't ramble, or make long speeches about your work, and don't argue with him or question his judgement. You may think you're better than him. Maybe you are better than him. But for the time being, he is sitting in his chair and you're sitting in yours.

If you disagree with something your CD says, phrase it as a question. For example, let's say he wants you to make a headline shorter. Don't say: *"That won't work."* Instead, ask: *"Do you think it still has the same meaning, without those words?"*

You've *got* to get on with this guy.

The single best predictor of success in any job is whether your boss likes you. And a creative department is no exception.

If your creative director likes you, he will spend more time with you, and you'll learn more about what he's looking for on a particular brief, and the kind of work he likes in general.

He may favor you with better briefs, be less likely to fire you if you under-perform, and be more likely to go along with your suggestions for photographers, directors, music, and the like.

He may even give you the benefit of the doubt when it comes to whether one of your ideas is any good or not.

Creative directors are like parents. They are in a position of immense power over their children, and it would be fairer and better if they liked them all equally, but in reality, they don't. That's just human nature. Out of any two people, you will always like one slightly better than the other.

Some CDs, like some parents, do play favorites. I have seen examples when a CD didn't buy an idea that a less-favored team showed him, but when the "teacher's pets" showed him virtually the same idea, he bought it.

Quite often, a CD will even *give* a team an idea. For free. This normally happens because the CD has thought of one himself, but hasn't got time to produce the ad. So he'll just suggest it to the first team that comes into his office. Or, more likely, to his favorites.

The sad fact is that a commitment to treating everyone equally is not a necessary qualification for being a CD.

And even the CD who is scrupulously fair-minded can't help but be unconsciously influenced. For example, when a CD buys your ad, he will then be spending a lot more time with you, while the ad gets produced. So if you're someone he unconsciously wants to spend more time with, he will unconsciously prefer to buy your ad rather than that of someone he doesn't like.

Now for the really bad news: you can't *make* your CD like you. (Sucking up backfires.)

This is no surprise—you can't *force anyone* in the world to like you. Perhaps you're a naturally likeable person. In which case, no problem. But perhaps you're not—perhaps you're shy, spiky, or surly. That still might not matter, if you have loads in common with this CD, or a similar sense of humor or way of looking at the world. But perhaps you don't.

In the case where there is no natural mutual fondness and not much in common either, the best you can do is make an extra effort to be friendly, hard-working, responsive to his requests, diligent, thoughtful, and a good listener. In other words, you can't make him like you, but you can make him like working with you.

HOW TO GET THE BEST OUT OF YOUR CD

So here's how to get the best out of your CD.

On a big project, or a complex one, go and see him as soon as you've been briefed—before you've even started work.

Ask him if he has a particular take on the brief, otherwise known as "a steer."

This can save a lot of time. He may have another campaign in mind as a tonal reference. He may already have an idea of his own. Also, don't forget to ask what he thinks would be *wrong* for this brief. Knowing what *not* to do can save you lots of time.

While you're working on the brief, try to get as much time with him as you can.

In addition to any scheduled reviews, pop in for an informal chat or two. The more time you spend with him at this stage, the better idea you'll have of what he's looking for.

I've already covered how to present to the CD in Chapter 5, but there's more to a successful review than presenting your work well. The main skill you will need is listening.

Every CD loves the sound of their own voice; the more you listen to him, the more he will think what great company you are. Plus, if you listen hard enough, he may tell you how to crack the brief. If you throw in the occasional insightful question, he may even crack the brief for you himself, "live."

If he asks you to do something specific for the next review, do it.

If you don't think it works, do something else as well—something better—but if you haven't at least done what he asked, he may get cross.

Don't argue. For some reason, it's a defining characteristic of CDs that they do not change their minds if you argue with them. That doesn't mean you can't get your way—far from it—but you just have to be subtle. An example of the wrong thing to say would be "*Well, the account team agrees with us*" or "*This is our ad and we just want to do it the way we want to do it.*"

Most CDs are control freaks and you *have* to make it look as if you are doing what he says. Even if you're not.

Let's take a common situation. You crack the brief early on, you know your idea is perfect for the brief, and the account team thinks so too, but for whatever reason, the creative director blows it out. What you do is wait until the client is screaming out for something, then you go back into the creative director, having made a few minor tweaks to your work, and tell him: "*Look, we took on board your comments about this, we've made a few changes, and we were wondering whether you think it works now?*" He can then approve it, thinking it was *his* input that saved the day.

Get to know each individual CD's style. Don't ask him directly "what his style is" because no one likes to think they have one. But they all do. Some CDs go for highly rational work, for example, and some prefer a more emotional approach.

The better you know your CD's tastes, the more work you will sell to him.

After whether your CD likes you, the next most important factor is whether he is any good.

A good CD makes a massive difference. Some CDs consistently get great work out, whatever the agency, whatever the client. It's no coincidence that the world's top CDs are paid five, ten, or 20 times what the average creative earns.

But if you happen to have a bad CD, the situation is not lost. After all, you can still come up with great work. It's just more of a challenge to get him to buy it.

HOW TO HANDLE THE DIFFERENT TYPES OF BAD CD

Here are some different types of bad CD, and how to handle them:

Indecisive. He asks you to show him option after option, like a princess in a shoe store. Just grit your teeth, and wait it out. In the end, he will probably pick the first thing you showed him.

Unconfident. He likes what you have done, but…he's not sure. If he's worried that the client won't go for it, you need to give him lots of reference, and good arguments, to help him sell it. If he's not sure whether it will be a good ad or not, get him excited about it. Tell him that other teams have come into your office, seen it, and raved about it. Talk about which other great ads it could be like, or which photographer or director you could get to shoot it.

Erratic. Today he loves your idea, tomorrow he wants another one. With a CD like this, it can be hard to keep your temper, and your sanity. The best approach is to use the account team, to make him define exactly what he's looking for. They can ask the nasty questions better than you can.

Client-friendly. Maybe he wants an easy life, maybe he's convinced himself (perhaps rightly) that this client will never buy great work, or maybe he's just an account man in disguise, who has got to the top by sucking up. Whatever the reason for his safety-first attitude, this type of CD can be the most frustrating of all. Probably your best chance of getting groundbreaking work through this character is to make it appear conventional. Base it around words or images that the product category habitually uses, but find a way to twist them into something exciting.

Perfectionist. He basically likes what you've done, but wants you to make endless tweaks. Solution: make the first round of changes and then get the traffic person to take him the work, rather than showing it to him yourself. Without you there to demonstrate his brilliance to, further fine-tuning becomes less fun for him.

Credit-hog. He feels that adding a couple of commas to your TV script gives him the right to add his name to the credits. Nothing you can do. Everyone in the industry knows who these people are; they are considered a joke. You haven't lost out, so just laugh it off.

Thieving. He takes your idea and rewrites the script as his own. Or he gives your idea to another team. This is tricky. He may have seen your idea and forgotten he's seen it—a genuine mistake. Use your knowledge of the person. If he's a good guy, then gently remind him that you already showed him that idea (have the script in your hand when you have the conversation) and you'll be fine. But if he's known for his larceny, then there's nothing you can do; he'll never own up to it. Work on your escape plan.

Egotistical. He wastes the first ten minutes of every review with a detailed run-down of what he did at the weekend, how hot his new nanny is, and where he's planning to go for lunch tomorrow. What you should do: smile. Things could be a lot worse. For one thing, he clearly likes you. If you're short of time, politely but firmly tell him you need this layout signed off straight away—the client is waiting in the meeting room and is about to have a brain hemorrhage.

Has issues. The known issues that can affect creative directors include: drug problems, alcohol problems, sexual addiction, mid-life crisis, depression, bipolar disorders, borderline personality disorders, and addictions to caffeine, sneakers, street art, and buying houses. If your CD has "issues," the best advice is to catch him on a good day. One agency was famous for having joint ECDs, one of whom was an alcoholic, the other a coke fiend. The solution the teams found was to show work to one of them in the morning; the other in the afternoon.

In general, if you have a bad CD, who doesn't like you, then you need to get another job as soon as you can.

If you have a good CD, who also likes you…then you are in a rare and happy position.

Hang on to it.

HOW TO GET THE BEST OUT OF PHOTOGRAPHERS AND ILLUSTRATORS

Advertising photographers have a great life. They normally ride a motorbike, and live/work in an enormous wood-floored studio in the trendiest part of town. For most of the year, they work on personal projects, like photographing the glaciers in Iceland, or gang culture in East L.A. And occasionally, they take photographs for advertisements.

The "occasionally" part is a problem. There are thousands of photographers out there. Even more than there are directors.

That's a big problem for them, because a lot of photographers don't get much work. And it's a problem for you too, because you have thousands of photographers to choose between.

Even more so than with directors, the most important aspect of getting the best result from a photographer is choosing the right one in the first place.

If your agency has an art buying department, or a head of art, make full use of them. In some agencies, it's compulsory for art directors to see the head of art and get his input before choosing a photographer. In most agencies, the system is less formal, but I would strongly recommend getting to know your head of art, and art buying department. The good ones have an encyclopedic knowledge of photographers and illustrators. Show them your layout, and ask who they would recommend for the job. Often, they'll give you a complete gem, and make you look like a genius. If you don't agree with their recommendation, you've lost nothing.

As a general rule, work with the most talented and experienced people you can. But don't be afraid to occasionally take a risk with untried talent—it could make your ad look more distinctive.

Choose a photographer on the strength of what they're good at. Sounds obvious, but art directors often choose a photographer because they love their work and then make them do something entirely different.

Some photographers and illustrators like to present themselves as good at lots of things, but this is an illusion. Every photographer has an essence to their work. If you're an art director, gaining a good working knowledge of these artists and their styles is a vital part of your job.

See photographers' reps when they call. Ask your art buyer regularly to show you interesting new work. Look at photography and illustration in magazines (editorial and ads) and find out who did them. Photocopy your favorites and keep them in a scrapbook. Go to galleries. Trawl the internet for interesting stuff and claim that you're working.

Nowadays, every photographer and illustrator has their portfolio online. Keep up with image-makers' websites, and know where people's heads are at.

"Don't get somebody to do what they did ten years ago," advises Mark Reddy, head of art at BBH in London.

"Get people doing what they want to do, as well as what you want to do."

Really study their portfolios and websites. Work out exactly what each does best and match that to what you want for your concept.

Don't be lazy and pick someone you've heard of, or who has just won an award. (Though if you do end up working with a famous photographer or illustrator, don't be overawed. Remember, it's a partnership.)

DON'T TYPE-CAST

Try not to fall into the trap of type-casting (e.g. getting a famous car photographer to do yet another car shoot). You can often get interesting results by not going with the obvious choice.

In fact, it's a classic laziness to choose someone who has shot a similar subject before. Don't worry too much about subject matter. In other words, if your ad features a horse on roller skates, there's no need to find a photographer who has previously shot roller-skating equines.

By understanding that a photographer's style is about more than his subject, you can make more exciting hirings: using a jewelry photographer to shoot a car, because they will make it look like an exquisite high-fashion item, for example.

The most important thing to look for in a photographer's book is a tone of voice that matches what you want for your ad. If you want your ad to be funny, look for a photographer who does funny. And again, narrow down as much as possible what kind of funny you want. Do you want surreal humor? Slapstick humor? Understated humor? There are so many photographers out there, the more you can decide in your own mind what you want, the more likely you are to find the perfect match.

A good match is vital. There's nothing more futile than trying to change a photographer's style to match your idea. It's the cause of a huge amount of friction between agency and client. Be honest about what the client needs, what your idea is about, and what the photographer or illustrator is best at; don't try to mash them together.

When you've got the right horse, the riding's easy. He won't try and go anywhere you don't want to go, and you won't have to use the whip.

Actually, the relationship between creatives and photographers (or illustrators) tends to be a lot less fraught than the relationship with directors. Perhaps it's because less money is being spent, so each job is less pressured. Perhaps it's because photographers tend to be more laid-back characters than directors.

If you've spent plenty of time talking about the job beforehand, then at the actual shoot you're just there as a fail-safe. One or two well-known art directors (Dave Dye, for example) don't even go on shoots.

"Have the confidence to stand back and let the illustrator/photographer get on with it," advises Grant Parker, head of art at DDB London. "Trust what they do, trust their talent. There is no point in commissioning someone, and then being too prescriptive about how they should do it."

"I prefer being able to give a photographer/illustrator a slightly looser brief so that they will come back with something a bit unexpected," he adds.

The trick is to strike the right balance between giving them a clear and accurate brief of what you want them to do, and leaving them enough creative freedom to add something of their own. This will keep them motivated, and hopefully get you a better image than you could have come up with by pressing the camera shutter yourself.

Leaving room for experiment often leads to happy accidents and surprising results. Which of course leads to more memorable ads.

"Don't have a preconceived notion of what you want the picture to look like," agrees Mark Reddy. *"The act of creating anything is a journey. Be open to let the idea develop."*

Running a photography shoot is less complex than running a film shoot. There's often no client or account team there. (Slight watch-out—no client on the set means you have to deliver a shot that conforms to the agreed layout, in addition to any other directions that might emerge over the course of the shoot.)

But in general, the same principles apply. Let them do what they want to do—what you hired them for. Only if they are going wrong should you intervene. Hanging back a bit will also give you some mental space, which allows other ideas to improve the shot to occur to you.

Most art directors really enjoy working with photographers and illustrators—it's often the bit of the job they like best. They enjoy actually making something; there's a real pleasure in the physicality of the process.

For the duration of the job, the art director is a patron, a collaborator, a fellow artist, and crucially… out of the office.

Get what you want from photographers by using a combination of charm, positive encouragement, enthusiasm, and *appearing* to compromise.

Be willing to bend on the things that aren't important—this buys you the right to stand firm on things that are.

"Disagreements and heated arguments are unnecessary," claims Paul Belford. *"I simply say 'let's try it both ways'."*

HOW TO GET THE BEST OUT OF TYPOGRAPHERS

For some reason, advertising agencies have decided that for film, the process involves going to an outside specialist—an external production company. But with print, it's nearly always done in-house.

In some smaller agencies, the art directors design the ads themselves.

In the larger and better agencies, there is a specialist studio, design, or typography department, whose responsibility it is to turn a photograph or illustration into a finished advertisement—deciding how to treat the image, selecting type for it, and bringing these elements harmoniously together.

There's some advantage to working with a pool of people that you know well. But the geographical closeness has a disadvantage too.

According to Mark Reddy, "The designers get seen as plumbers who just do what they're told." Plus "sometimes there are about 16 people around a monitor. Nothing can get done then. And anyone in the agency can come up and sit on their shoulder…account handlers, planners, anyone…and make a comment."

Therefore, one of the roles of the art director is to protect the designer.

In general, the relationship between an art director and the studio tends to be rather good. After all, there's so much common ground. The studio guys are normally people who love great images and good design, just like art directors.

(For some reason, designers are nearly always into music too. It's almost impossible for some of them to even begin working on a design until they have selected the correct iTunes playlist to accompany it.)

Most designers are cool, laid-back people that art directors find easy to get along with. But design is subjective. In a studio that employs several designers, you are bound to prefer the work of some over others.

So once again, the best way to get the best out of your studio is to pair your job with the right designer in the first place. Some in-house guys are jacks-of-all-trades, so their personal style won't either particularly benefit or fight with your project. But some will have their own style.

Some will be the hip ones, into funky ways to use type, or outrageous ways to crop an image. Others will obsess over every detail, and produce tightly controlled layouts. Find the one who's right for your job. You will soon get to know this. But if you're a new art director or new to the agency, ask for advice from your traffic person or the head of the studio.

AN ASSIGNED TYPOGRAPHER

If you don't have a choice, but instead your job is "assigned" to a typographer, then you need to behave differently according to whether you have been assigned to a good typographer, or a not-so-good one.

Put simply, you give the good typographer more freedom—a clear brief, but which is wide enough to allow them to add their own input. Ask them for their own ideas too. With the weaker typographer, you'll have to be very specific about what you want. They won't add anything to your idea, but even the less creative typographers should be able to competently execute your thinking, and as long as you don't expect them to add any of their own, you can still be satisfied with their work.

Actually, it's important in general that you don't confuse a designer with an art director. It's not their responsibility to come up with an overall art direction idea for an ad; it's yours.

AND GIVE THEM TIME...

Some art directors make the mistake of going into the studio too early.

"*Whatever you do,*" says Paul Belford, "*don't just hand over a scrap of paper with a scribble on it and say: 'Do something interesting with this please'.*"

Even if you know the style you want, say for example you want something "cool" for an ad promoting your city's night bus service, don't brief your designer to "do something cool." That's a dreadful brief. It's too wide. You need to have an idea first, for example, if you are trying to make the night bus a cool mode of transportation for young people, you might have the idea of art directing your ad like a nightclub flyer.

Then you need to find lots of reference for that. Allow time for the designer to find some too. Now he can riff off your idea, produce multiple styles of flyer, and the two of you can work out how the idea works best.

"*If you absolutely have to follow some turgid brand guidelines, be up-front about it,*" advises Paul Belford, "*so you don't waste time.*"

Time is vital. Give your designer as much of it as you can—don't expect something brilliant in an afternoon.

And as far as the final result goes, "*have an open mind and be prepared to be shocked,*" says Belford. "*If you're shocked, consumers will also be shocked. You want your work to get noticed, don't you?*"

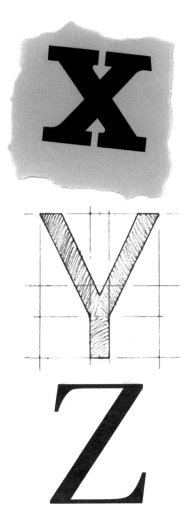

THRIVING

CHAPTER 7
MANAGING YOUR CAREER

HOW TO SPOT THE GOOD BRIEFS

If your advertising career is to thrive, the main thing you'll need (apart from being good) is good briefs to work on.

A good brief is one that offers the chance of doing great work. Often, it's "who it's for" that makes a brief an opportunity. Certain clients such as Volkswagen, Sony, Nike, Adidas, Levi's, and Budweiser buy outstanding work all over the world, year after year. (There are also certain brands that regularly do great work in one country only—like Harvey Nichols and *The Economist* in the UK; Skittles and Burger King in the US.)

Your agency may not have any of these particular accounts, but it will still have one or two clients that buy award-winning work, or at least do work that is interesting.

Traditionally, great work comes more often in certain categories—beer, cars, and sportswear spring to mind. Whether that's because these brands primarily target blokes and it's largely blokes on awards juries...I wouldn't like to say.

AND SPOT THE DOGS

As well as knowing what the good accounts are, you have to know which are your agency's dogs. The toilet cleaners, athlete's foot treatments, and shampoo accounts are usually, how can I put it, "creatively challenged"?

All creatives *claim* they like a challenge, but given the choice between a brief that's a huge challenge and another that's a massive opportunity, they'll pick the opportunity every time. In other words, they take Nike over the toilet cleaner ten times out of ten. Of course, the person who does the first great piece of advertising for a brand that's never previously had any gains great kudos. But the odds are looooooooooooooooooooong.

LOOKING FOR THE OPPORTUNITIES

In some cases, an account throws up a mixture of good and bad briefs. For example, a supermarket might do eight or ten super-dull "value" ads and one sumptuous brand ad a year.

Also, an average brand can suddenly present a good opportunity if a planner comes up with a really interesting strategy for it, or if sales dip and they need to do something dramatic.

The amount of money the client spends makes a difference too.

Maybe it shouldn't, but it does. Car brands spend big; that means they are important to the agency, the agency puts their top people on the account and good ads get made. Everyone likes to work on the accounts with big production budgets. Money isn't everything, and is not essential for producing great work, but if you do have it, then you have the choice of whether to spend it or not. Money gives you options.

There's an inherent media bias also, in that creatives tend to get more excited by TV briefs than any other kind. Next on the list is typically posters, followed by print, digital, and radio. Individual preferences may vary, of course.

The final factor is timing. If a brief has been in the agency for a long time, and hasn't been cracked, and the client is now desperate, then that's a good time to work on it. Conversely, if there is plenty of time on a project, then there's plenty of time to waste before anything needs to happen. Avoid.

Above all, don't believe what any account handler, planner, or traffic person says about a brief. They'll *always* tell you it's great. They will always tell you the client wants to do something really different on this one. And they will always tell you that the ECD has requested you personally for it. You can't blame them for wanting to get you excited about the project—they're just doing their job. But you must use your own judgement, and exercise caution.

HOW TO GET ASSIGNED BETTER BRIEFS

Having said all that, few creatives get the choice of whatever briefs they want to work on. Some creatives, particularly in the US, and particularly on larger accounts, may be permanently assigned to a certain client. Most CDs are. The average creative "floats" but that doesn't mean he's "free;" it just means he can be assigned to any project for any client in the building.

And if there's one process within an agency that's frustratingly mysterious to creatives, it is the question of how briefs are assigned. Nearly all creatives believe they aren't getting fair treatment, and fear that another team down the hall is getting all the best briefs.

They probably are. Although no ECD would admit it, there's a pecking order in any creative department. Sometimes an exciting brief might go to both a senior and a junior team, to see what they each come up with. But usually the "top teams" get the big brand TV spots, and the junior or lesser-rated teams get the trade ads.

Hence if you are a young team, just starting out, you will probably be given less prestigious briefs at first. This may seem unfair, but from the agency's point of view, they want the projects that are high-profile and high-stakes to go to their most experienced teams, since it's more important that the agency gets them right.

If you aren't such a young team any more, an easy way to tell how you stand within an agency is simply by the quality of the briefs you are getting. If you aren't getting good briefs, then they don't rate you. It's that simple, I'm afraid.

However, it's not terminal. The solution is the same, whatever your age, whatever your level of experience. Try to shine on the briefs you're assigned to, but work on the more exciting briefs as well, unofficially. If your entire day is taken up with your official briefs, then you may need to work evenings and weekends if you want to progress.

A very few agencies don't like teams working on briefs they're not officially assigned to. If that is the case, only show work if you're sure it's brilliant—brilliant enough to make them forget you "stole" the brief.

But most agencies are delighted if teams work on a brief unofficially—it gives them more options. Just follow the house rules on how discreet you have to be.

Not many workplaces are as meritocratic as an ad agency. Do the job on a few of the agency's high-profile projects and you will zoom up the hierarchy, scoring better and better briefs as you go.

And if you never want to get a bad brief again, keep cracking the good ones.

WORKING OUT WHICH MEDIUM IS RIGHT FOR YOU

THE HIERARCHY OF MEDIA

As your career progresses, you may focus on different media.

Typically, a beginning team gets mostly print, radio, and digital briefs, before "graduating" to TV.

There's a perception that TV is harder.

And there is some truth in that. For one thing, there are simply more steps in the process of a TV shoot—like editing and grading—which aren't part of a print shoot.

There's more to learn.

The budget is also bigger for a TV ad, so it's higher pressure. There are more people involved, so it's more complicated. And there are more levels of approval to get through, both on the client side and in the agency (sometimes it's more difficult getting a big TV ad through your agency than through the client—the managing director, head of planning, chairman…they all want a say in the TV, but for some reason, not the radio). Senior teams have more experience of dealing with this kind of pressure and politics; hence creative directors prefer senior teams for big TV ads.

THE HIERARCHY OF BRIEF-DIFFICULTY

As well as this unofficial hierarchy of media, there's a hierarchy of brief-difficulty too. The hardest brief is for a new brand campaign, since it normally involves heavy-duty strategic thinking (e.g. *"What should T-Mobile stand for?"*). Product briefs are a little easier, since the brand personality has already been established, and you're only devising the strategy for one product, not a whole brand (e.g. *"How do we advertise T-Mobile's new Pay Monthly package?"*). The next easiest are "offer" ads (*"15% off T-Mobile's new Pay Monthly package"*) and the easiest of all are tactical ads (ads used "tactically" to capitalize on a specific event or occasion, e.g. *"15 percent off T-Mobile's new Pay Monthly package if you sign up on April 1st—genuine offer, not an April Fool!"*).

You'll notice the difficulty is in proportion to how open the brief is. The question of what T-Mobile should stand for, for example, has hundreds of possible answers, so the CD would assign this brief to one of his most experienced teams, because he trusts they will hunt high and low to find a good one. But since *"15 percent off when you sign up on April 1st"* is much more limiting, with maybe only one or two possible angles, he's more happy to assign it to a junior team.

Other supposedly "easier" briefs could include a small-space print ad, a trade ad, a digital banner, or a tactical radio ad. While these briefs can sometimes present good opportunities, there are fewer creative options available, which does make them more straight-forward. And these are the sorts of briefs most teams start off with.

VARIETY AND PREFERENCE

Having said the above, many CDs like to put both a senior team and a junior one on a big brand TV ad. They reason that while the senior team is more likely to crack it, the junior team may come up with something fresher.

This means that while you may find yourself doing some big TV ads quite early in your career, a more typical path is for teams to do more print at the beginning and more TV later.

Along the way, you may develop a preference for one particular medium. Some creatives just love the instant hit of the poster. Some are interactive gurus who have little time for "old media." And one leading radio writer told me he gravitated toward that medium because he had *"the visual sense of Blind Lemon Jefferson."*

If you feel a strong pull toward one medium, you may want to consider a career as a specialist. For example, in many countries there are specialist radio production houses, or pure digital agencies.

But even generalists—and that's most creatives—are allowed to have a favorite medium. Some creatives are regarded as "digital natives" or "a great print team," but still do everything.

The only caveat is that if you want to become a creative director, it definitely helps to have proved your ability across a variety of media. There's a feeling that if you've never done a good TV ad, how can a team take you seriously when you're advising them how to make theirs better?

BRIEFS
(IN ORDER OF DIFFICULTY)

· New brand campaign
· Product brief
· "Offer ads"
· Tactical ads

SELF-INITIATED PROJECTS OR CHIP SHOP ADS

A few years ago, there was a spate of award-winning ads in the UK for chip shops. One example famously featured the magnificent USP that *"Other fish 'n' chip shops don't give a fork."*

Why did the nation's chip shops suddenly (and simultaneously) request witty, highly creative advertising? The answer is that they didn't. What happened was that these ads were created by creative teams for the sole purpose of their own self-advancement—i.e. to win awards—and the mini-boom in fried-takeaway advertising led to such work being dubbed "chip shop ads." Another term for the practice is scam ads or, in some countries, ghost ads.

If a legitimate ad is defined as one that had a proper airing in legitimate media, then I would estimate that at least a third of the adverts that win lions in the press and poster categories at Cannes are scam.

TYPES OF SCAM

The most common scam is when an agency creates a press ad for a client, and then "accidentally" enters it into the poster awards as well.

Another widespread scam is when an agency proposes a campaign for one of its clients, and the client loves it—except for one execution, which they despise. This is usually the bravest and most interesting one. To keep the agency happy, the client agrees to run this additional execution in one publication only; purely so it qualifies for entry to awards (ads that haven't run can't be entered). This is *almost* a legitimate ad. It was requested by the client, approved by the client, paid for by the client, and genuinely appeared in the media. However, the definition does become a little stretched when a super-sexy ad for a luxury 4x4 turns up in a knitting magazine, because the client didn't want to splash out for space in a more suitable (and expensive) publication. Or when an additional TV ad that the client didn't like, that was shot at the same time as the ones they did like, runs at 3am on the fishing channel. Believe me, this happens a lot.

These "self-initiated" ads are my own. In both cases the client approved the executions and paid for them to appear, so I'd argue they are on the right side of the spec vs scam dividing line.

And it gets worse. What if a client refuses to pay for the ad to run? The agency pays. And if the client hates the ad so much, they won't approve it to run at all? The agency pays for it to run, and doesn't tell the client it has. Sometimes, an agency makes an ad for one of its clients, pays for the ad to run, and enters it into awards schemes, all without the client even being aware of its existence.

That's a bit like someone stealing your dog, giving it an extreme makeover, and entering it for a dog show… all without you knowing it's left the house.

Sounds crazy, but there are highly publicized cases that fit exactly that template.

In 2008, a TV commercial for the JC Penney clothing store was awarded a Bronze Lion at Cannes. The only problem was that JC Penney had never seen the script, didn't know the ad was being shot, hadn't paid for it to run, and only discovered its existence when they heard it had won the Lion, at which point they became furious, since the ad's subject matter—it showed two teens "speed undressing"—did not reflect the chain's wholesome family values. The Lion was returned.

For years there's been a rumor that one highly award-winning agency has an entire "shadow department" of creative teams dedicated solely to producing scam ads. The creatives working on the agency's real clients are said to sit on a separate floor, and aren't even allowed to talk to the "just for Cannes" teams.

This story is probably made up. But it gets told and retold, like an ad industry "urban myth," because it taps into a genuine fear—that our industry is riddled with scam. And let's face it, the awards schemes are full of 48-sheet posters for dog obedience classes and language schools—ads that were created by creatives on their Macs, specifically to win awards, which were never approved by any client, and almost certainly never ran.

Nancy Vonk, co-chief creative officer of Ogilvy Toronto, told *Creativity* magazine:

"Scams taint every show and burn clients at a time when there is a bigger appetite to endorse award-winning work. It's an unfortunate burden on those who have to keep an eye out for anything that smells fishy. So: bar the agency with their name on the scam from entering the show the next year. Display scams prominently on the awards show site for public shaming. And all entries need a client signature in the first place. This wouldn't solve everything; it's a pain and the shows would have to be OK with losing the next year's entry fees. But any answer to this is going to hurt."

Some countries are worse for scams than others. I once served on an advertising awards jury with another juror who was from Singapore. He explained to me that he wouldn't be voting for any ads at all from his own country, because he "knew" they were all scam. India and Thailand are also getting a bad reputation. An Asia-based CD admits:

"There's no doubt that a few people here have built healthy careers on the back of print ads that the client would barely recognize. They'd justify it in a number of ways: raising the standards of advertising in backward local markets; showing potential clients what the agency is capable of; and the need to compete creatively with Europe and America on far smaller budgets."

However, he contends that scamming is less prevalent now than it used to be.

"It's unfortunate that there's so much suspicion about Asian print work now, since it means some work is unfairly dismissed as scam, when it's genuine."

In actual fact, no country is immune. Plenty of scam ads come out of the UK, US, Australia, and Germany.

A MORAL ISSUE?

The industry is split on the morality of the scam issue. Some view it as a harmless way for ambitious creatives, who feel they're not getting sufficient creative opportunities on their agency's existing clients, to showcase their talent. Others view it simply as cheating. They liken it to the problem of drugs in sport, and argue that every award that goes to a scam ad means an award being taken away from a team that has played by the rules.

This book is not a work of moral philosophy, so I'm not going to advise you on what you should and shouldn't do. However, I will tell you what I personally feel to be sensible and acceptable practice.

First of all, if your agency has many clients that offer good creative opportunities, then you shouldn't be trying to do scam ads at all. What I mean is that if you are working at Abbott Mead Vickers in London, why would you waste your time approaching the local chip shop when *The Economist* has such a great advertising heritage and is constantly crying out for great posters?

But if your agency does not have any good clients, then you are quite within your rights to go out and get one yourself. Actually, the whole exercise can be really good fun.

HOW TO MAKE A SPEC AD

1 First of all, think of a great idea for an advert. It's often easiest if it's a print ad, just because costs are lower in print and it's easier to pull favors, but it could also be for TV or ambient.

2 Next, get it shot. That's right; you get it shot *before* you show the client. That's because you only want the ad to get made exactly how you want it—your vision, free from all the usual compromises. For a print ad, the best way to do this is to find a hungry young photographer who is happy to shoot something for free. You can even get a TV ad shot for free—ask your TV department if they know of any young directors looking to make "test films." Many production companies are actively looking to put money into getting a test film shot, because if it comes out great, it can launch a director's reputation, and lead to high-paying glamorous jobs for him.

3 Because you want to make the ad before you show it to a client, make sure you choose a category that has many potential clients. I once shot a spec ad for a bed store, based around the territory of "beds so comfortable, you'll never have a nightmare again." The first image depicted a typical nightmare—being trouserless in public. At the first bed store we took it to, the manager liked the idea. Hence the name on the bottom of the ad became Alphabeds. However, if Alphabeds hadn't liked it, the ad could have worked equally well for BettaBeds or Comfort Beds.

4 But if you had come up with an ad campaign for the Tower of London, say, based on the idea of "the most remarkable tower since Babel," then if the people at the Tower of London don't like it, you are in trouble, since there is no other tourist attraction in London that is also a tower.

If a friend of yours has a store or a small business, then so much the better. Go see them. Yes, it's slightly easier to sell a campaign when the client is your mate or your uncle…but for me, that's not cheating, it merely replicates real-world conditions—every agency finds it easier to sell to clients they are good friends with.

But if you don't know anyone, it doesn't matter. Any pet store or local hairdresser will be surprised and delighted to be offered a free ad campaign. Just ring them up. It's not nearly as hard as it sounds, and it's actually great fun to be your own account handler for a change. On the understanding that they will pay for the ad to run at least once in legitimate media, you let the client have the artwork at no cost.

Only once the whole campaign is signed, sealed, and delivered do you tell your creative director about the project. Hopefully, the ad has come out well and he will be happy to put the agency's name to it. Bringing it under the agency's wing is important, because you want the agency to pay the (considerable) costs of awards entries.

Don't forget to PR it too. Because this isn't a normal agency project with all the machinery of an account team behind it, it's up to you to talk through the campaign with your agency's PR person. Or simply send it out yourself to the trade press, *Archive* magazine, and the ad blogs.

Getting awards and PR gives you a maximum return on your effort. But even if those don't come off, you'll still have a great ad for your book, and you'll learn as much as you would on six normal campaigns—so it's definitely worth doing. But only in the early years of your career.

If you're still doing spec ads at age 35, something has gone wrong.

PITCHES

While some clients show huge loyalty—for example, Ogilvy has handled the advertising for American Express since 1962—others change agency more often than P. Diddy changes his name.

Reasons include a client unhappy with the agency's work, a breakdown in relationship between the two parties, or a new marketing director who wants to take the brand in a new direction.

Agency bosses wine and dine clients who they think might one day put their business up for pitch, and buy them Christmas presents. One agency I know buys Christmas *trees*. Fully loaded.

Pitches are incredibly important to an advertising agency. There's a perception that if an agency isn't growing, it's dying.

And since people who work in advertising are highly competitive, pitches get their juices flowing. The proof is that their second question—right after "what are we pitching for?" is always "who are we up against?"

However, fundamentally, creatives want to make ads. And the work produced for a pitch rarely ends up getting made. Pitch work is intended as a demonstration of the kind of work the agency *could* do, and no one really expects a new brand campaign to be cracked in two weeks.

Sure, there's an excitement to a pitch, a camaraderie. Plus there's usually a big night out to celebrate the pitch coming to an end…and an even bigger one if you win. But many creatives resent the late nights, cold pizza, and time wasted when they could have been making real ads.

I'm sure agency managing directors would be utterly appalled to read this, and would rain blows on me like a piñata if they thought I was advising creatives not to try hard on pitches.

Luckily, I'm not. Pitches are so important to the agency in general, you *must* put a big effort in, or be seen as a dangerous anarchist. Put any concerns that it's a waste of time right to the back of your mind, and go all out to win.

The biggest contribution a creative can make to winning a pitch is to come up with "a line."

Clients often deny they want a line, agencies claim they're not trying to think of one, and consumers are rarely interested in them when they appear.

And yet the power of a single sentence, which sums up what an entire brand stands for...

What could Guinness say to Abbott Mead Vickers after they showed them "Good Things Come To Those Who Wait" other than thank you, here's our money, please go and make the campaign?

AWARDS

John O'Keeffe, global CD of the WPP group, once went to a restaurant in Cannes, and liked their steak-frites so much he returned the next night. But this time, the bill had doubled. When O'Keeffe queried it, the waiter explained "*Monsieur, the festival 'as begun.*"

The people who organize Cannes, D&AD, The One Show, and the Clios, charge advertising agencies hundreds of dollars to enter each piece of work. To order an extra Cannes lion (e.g. for the client) costs $1150. And as discussed, some agencies spend a fortune entering work that was especially created for awards shows, and never ran in the real world.

Even the way awards are determined is occasionally corrupt, with work from jury members' own agencies getting a suspiciously large share.

However, if you want to have a successful career, you need to win awards.

The times in my career when I got a pay rise all followed winning awards. The times when headhunters contacted me about jobs at other agencies followed winning awards. The times when I started to get better briefs all followed winning awards too.

And I'm no special case. The evidence for the importance of awards is as solid as the evidence for evolution or gravity.

Just walk around any creative department and look at people's shelves. Generally, the ECD has the most awards. Then the creative directors. Then the senior teams. Then the middleweights. And then the juniors. In other words, the more awards you have, the higher up the hierarchy you rise. More money, more responsibility, more opportunities.

That is fact.

SHOULD AWARDS BE AS IMPORTANT AS THEY ARE?

The question of whether awards *should* have the importance they do is a completely separate one.

It's commonly stated, for example, that creatives ought not to care about awards, but effectiveness. Personally, I find it annoying that this debate is still going on, since study after study has shown an extremely strong correlation between award-winning work and effective work. Also, whether an ad works or not is a function of so many things other than its creative quality—for example, the strategy may be wrong, or the media placement flawed.

Asking for creatives to be judged on effectiveness is like asking strikers to be judged on the number of clearances they make in their own penalty area. Yes, it's great if a striker can do that. But they must primarily be judged on their goals.

Some say awards exist because advertising creatives have egos the size of hot-air balloons. Again, I think that's unfair. There are awards in the movie industry, the car industry…for all I know, there's an award for accountant and doctor of the year as well.

And awards are arguably more necessary in our business than in certain other human endeavors such as athletics, motor racing, and typing contests, which offer a simple way to see who the winner is—the first person to finish. Advertising doesn't have an objective measure like that.

And since the jury system is good enough for judging murder trials, it ought to be good enough for judging adverts. Of course the potential for anomalies exists, as with any jury. But because the question of "*What is good work?*" will always be a matter of opinion, it seems to me that referring to a jury of experts in the field is, while imperfect, the best system we are going to get.

Some creatives (and some agencies) don't care about awards at all. They view them as solid-metal tokens of our insecurity; and they may be right.

But whether they really are a valid way of judging creatives' merits or not, they *are* what the industry will judge you on.

WHAT WORK WINS AWARDS?

So if awards are that important, how do you win them?

There is absolutely no mystery about the type of work that juries go for.

And these criteria are typically the ones any creative would tell you make for an outstanding piece of communication: simple, engaging, impactful, rewarding, relevant, original, and produced to a high executional standard.

Some creatives complain there's a "formula" to award-winning work—like a print ad that consists of nothing but an image with a visual twist, and the client's logo placed small in the corner.

It's probably true that there's a certain type of work that does well at Cannes—the juries are international, hence work that is purely visual and requires no understanding of foreign languages or cultures will connect with more judges.

You could view this type of work as non-groundbreaking. Perhaps it is. Nevertheless, if it represents a really first-class example of our craft, then I don't see any reason why it shouldn't win awards.

However, the type of work that wins the truly prestigious awards (e.g. Cannes Grand Prix, D&AD Gold) is often work that genuinely is groundbreaking. That means it doesn't follow the usual formulas, but redefines its medium, or its category, in some way.

For example, the poster campaign for Britain's National Gallery, which won a rare "black pencil" at D&AD in 2008, didn't use conventional posters at all, but instead took the artworks themselves out into the streets of London…

PAY

Writing adverts. It's a tough job, but somebody has to do it.

And of course, that somebody is not going to do it for free.

Peter Mayle, a former ad-man who has since found fame as the author of *A Year in Provence*, describes how he felt when he was offered his first creative directorship. *"I decided to give it a go,"* he says. *"It was exciting to have been elevated so quickly. I was only 26, I was earning twice what the prime minister got paid, and I owned a house on Sloane Square."*

Wonderful story.

But that was 1965.

Since then, house prices have gone north, and advertising salaries have gone south. The reasons are too depressing to go into, but suffice it to say, the days when creatives drove Ferraris are long gone.

The book *Freakonomics* describes advertising as a *"second-tier glamour profession"* (behind movies, sports, music, and fashion). But the way salaries are heading, I fear we may soon reach Tier 3.

People who work in advertising still earn, on average, a pretty decent wage. Less than bankers, lawyers, or management consultants; more than plumbers, teachers, or journalists.

However, in the early days of your career, you should be aware that you will earn much less than all the above-mentioned.

Why? As Steven D. Levitt and Stephen J. Dubner describe so brilliantly in *Freakonomics*, entrants to glamour industries;

"throw themselves at grunt jobs that pay poorly and demand unstinting devotion. An editorial assistant earning $22,000 at a Manhattan publishing house, an unpaid high-school quarterback, and a teenage crack dealer earning $3.30 an hour are all playing the same game, a game that is best viewed as a tournament."

"The rules of a tournament are straightforward. You must start at the bottom to have a shot at the top...You must be willing to work long and hard at substandard wages. In order to advance in the tournament, you must prove yourself not merely above average but spectacular."

IN OTHER WORDS

PEOPLE ARE WILLING TO EARN PEANUTS AT THE BOTTOM, BECAUSE THEY KNOW THE REWARDS FOR REACHING THE TOP ARE SO HIGH.

BUT JUST HOW HIGH ARE THEY?

ECD	250	– 500K
CREATIVE DIRECTOR	85	– 250K
GROUP HEAD	75	– 150K
SENIOR CREATIVE	60	– 125K
MIDDLEWEIGHT	30	– 75K
JUNIOR	18	– 30K

THESE ARE THE FIGURES FROM HEADHUNTERS, THE TALENT BUSINESS FOR ABOVE-THE-LINE CREATIVES IN LONDON, IN 2008.

OTHER MARKETS MAY VARY.
YOU'LL NOTICE THE BANDS ARE RATHER LARGE. THAT'S BECAUSE THERE ARE PLENTY OF TEAMS WITH THE SAME LEVEL OF ABILITY, AND THE SAME EXPERIENCE, BUT EARNING VASTLY DIFFERENT AMOUNTS...PURELY BECAUSE ONE TEAM WAS BETTER AT NEGOTIATING.

LIE ABOUT YOUR SALARY

The first couple of times I moved job, I failed to lie about my salary. Big mistake.

In each case, the CD asked us what we were earning, and then offered us a small increase over that—about 5 percent more—giving some excuse about how budgets were tight, but if we joined on this initially rather low amount, he would find more money for us soon.

What I later learned is that creative directors *assume you are lying* about your salary—to the tune of 15–30 percent. So they actually thought they were giving us a healthy raise.

What this means is that even if you are an extremely honest person, you really have to lie...simply because that's how the system works.

There's another school of thought that suggests you don't disclose your current salary, but simply ask to be paid what you're worth, rather than what your current agency is underpaying you.

Of course, if a CD asks your current salary, and you point-blank refuse to say, he may get annoyed. A direct question does probably necessitate a direct answer. But that's not to say it has to be an honest one. Ask yourself how much you deserve (honestly) and then add another 30 percent. If you do deserve it, you'll probably get knocked down to somewhere near what you really wanted.

I think a lot of creatives don't bargain hard enough because, aside from the fact that we're not natural negotiators like account handlers or real estate agents, we worry that we'll scare a CD away if we quote too high a figure. But actually, that won't happen.

The creative director can always try to bargain you down. And yet it's hard for you to bargain him up.

There was some excellent advice on how to negotiate your salary in the 2008 *Global Planning Survey*—they asked bosses for tips on what works. Here are the best ten:

1 Consider the total package. Think about where the job is going. The holiday allowance. The other benefits.
2 Get everything in writing.
3 Don't come off as entitled and push too hard for big salaries when you are junior.
4 For your first job, take what you can get.
5 Sadly, you have to jump around to make more money.
6 Women need to be stronger and firmer, and ask for what they want even if it feels uncomfortable.
7 Never tell your current salary. You deserve what your skills and talent pull in that market, not what looks better next to your old salary.
8 Negotiate hard. Creatives need to see a decent wage as a right rather than an indulgence. Realize that your hard and good work is making a profit for someone else.
9 Don't keep going back and forth. The boss's second offer is his best offer. After that he just gets pissed off.
10 Don't be the first to suggest a number.

Final word—the bad agencies normally pay more than the good ones. They have to.

Think hard about what you need most at this stage of your career—great money, or great opportunities.

HOURS

Is success due to talent, or working hard?

There's a widespread belief that "a natural talent for it" is essential for success in creative fields—like art, music, and advertising—far more so than in less creative fields like banking, accountancy, or law.

But is there any truth to that?

In Malcolm Gladwell's *Outliers* he explains something he calls the *"10,000 hour rule,"* which states that to become expert at *anything*, one simply needs to put in 10,000 hours practising it.

The 10,000 figure comes from the research of Anders Ericsson, who in the early 1990s studied violinists at the Berlin Academy of Music.

"The curious thing about Ericsson's study is that he and his colleagues couldn't find any "naturals"— musicians who could float effortlessly to the top while practising a fraction of the time that their peers did," writes Gladwell. "Nor could they find "grinds," people who worked harder than everyone else and yet just didn't have what it takes to break into the top ranks. Their research suggested that once you have enough ability to get into a top music school, the thing that distinguishes one performer from another is how hard he or she works. That's it. What's more, the people at the very top don't just work much harder than everyone else. They work much, much harder."

Some creatives cling to the belief that success is down to luck—getting the right brief at the right time, from a client that just happened to be looking for great work.

But if that is your view, you'll be in a minority. The pop culture quote: *"The harder I work, the luckier I get,"* attributed variously to movie mogul Sam Goldwyn and golfer Gary Player, has by now gained general acceptance.

So even if you personally disagree with Gladwell's theory that success is primarily due to hard work, you should certainly be aware that most people agree with it.

Which means that when you start a new job, it's vital you establish a reputation as a hard worker—arrive before your boss arrives, and don't leave until after he leaves. There's an old saying that goes: *"The man who has a reputation as an early riser, can get up at whatever time he chooses."*

If you are naturally a hard worker, my advice is don't work hard gratuitously. Take your full holiday entitlement, and take your weekends—unless there's a screaming emergency—else you'll either burn out, fall out of love with the business, or end up depriving yourself of essential external stimulation, and your work will suffer. It's easy to get into the habit of always leaving the office late as a matter of course. Don't do that. Keep an extra gear in reserve, so you can kick up your work-rate when there's a major crisis, or a major opportunity.

FOLLOW THE PREVAILING CULTURE

The question of how hard you should work is partly answered by the prevailing culture of the agency you're working at.

In some agencies, everyone works hard. *"If you don't come in on Saturday, then don't bother coming in on Sunday"*—words supposedly said by Tim Delaney, co-founder of UK hotshop Leagas Delaney. Wieden & Kennedy has such a reputation for long hours that it has acquired the nickname "Weekend & Kennedy." If you don't work hard in an agency like this, you'll have a double problem—not only will you not produce as much work as everyone else, but also, you won't fit in.

There are plenty of agencies where creatives generally work normal office hours. If that feels like what you want to do—perhaps you have a family or other interests, you're just not that into advertising, or you're mentally exhausted by six o'clock—then you'll be a lot happier if you work at one of these places.

But be aware that even at the "normal hours" shops, there are still plenty of times when you will have to work abnormal hours. Nearly every account goes into crisis from time to time, requiring late-night working for the early-morning meeting. And pitches eat weekends.

It must also be said that advertising is a job that can prey on your mind outside office hours. When I'm working on a brief, it gives me a kind of psychological eczema that I find myself scratching in the shower, on the bus, and on the toilet.

If you're looking for a 9 to 5 job, this probably isn't it.

WHEN TO MOVE AGENCIES

People are normally tempted to move for one of three reasons: more money, more opportunity, or they just fancy a change.

MORE MONEY

All of these reasons are valid. But one of them—the finance factor—is almost never mentioned. In every interview you'll ever read in an advertising trade magazine, a creative-on-the-move will talk about the "exciting new challenge" he's been offered.

He'll never say *"Look, the money was just amazing. Like, I mean really amazing."*

Nevertheless, money is a motivator. Of course it is. We all have bills to pay, and as creatives get older, some have ex-wives and school fees to pay. And for a young creative, the difference of just a few thousand pounds a year can mean the difference between a clean apartment in a safe part of town, and a hole with forms of insect life not yet known to science. So I don't devalue the importance of money as a motivation. And I always advise people that if you can get a job at an agency as good as your current one, but for more money, then take it.

It's the job of a boss to pay you as little as possible. That's just how capitalism works—if they paid everyone what they were worth, there would be no profit margin. You will be at your best-paid when you move jobs, because that is when you get your market value. Then, gradually, your pay starts to fall behind again. So if income is important to you, you need to move regularly to maximize it. And the best time to maximize is when you have just won an award or two. That is when your market value will be at its peak.

One thing to bear in mind though—every time you make a move, you're taking a risk. However well you know an agency from the outside, there will always be things that surprise you when you get on the inside. They may not be things that you like. However well you get on with the ECD at your interview, he might not be the same when you're working there. He might be better. But he might be worse. You just don't know for sure. Similarly, you can never be certain that your style of work will be right for the agency, or that you'll fit in there.

So make sure the additional income they are offering is enough to discount this "risk factor."

The question of whether to take more money to work at a *less* good agency…is a difficult one. The answer depends on how your career is going.

If you're still on the way up, you probably should *not* take the money. The reason for this is that, even if money was your sole motivation (which I'm sure it isn't), you wouldn't be maximizing your income over your whole career if you did that. You would get a short-term gain, but may lose out in the longer term, by denying yourself the opportunity to do the truly great work that could send your income soaring.

"Never make a decision based on coin," is how Fallon legend, Bob Barrie puts it.
"Do brilliant work and you'll be rewarded more in the end anyway."

However, if you're on the way down, either because you've lost the magic, drink too much, prefer to spend time with your family rather than in the office—or whatever the reason may be—then it may be the right thing to take the money. Senior creatives talk (in private) about "cashing in." After eight, ten, or 15 years of busting a gut to create excellent advertising at the best agencies around, there comes a time when you may want to take your foot off the gas, work at a slightly less good agency where there's less pressure creatively, and where you can command a large salary. Nothing wrong with that. There's more to your life than your career.

MORE OPPORTUNITY

The second reason for moving—more opportunity—is more straightforward. If you can get a similar job at a better agency, you should. It's probably not worth moving to an agency that's only a *little bit* better (remember, there's the risk factor I mentioned earlier to consider), but if you can go up to a new level, you should do so. Don't let fear hold you back. If you're good enough to get a job there, you're good enough to do well there.

Some people wonder whether it's worth taking a pay cut for a job at a better agency. It is. The likelihood is that the short-term salary drop is soon overtaken by the greater rewards that come from doing better work.

The only caveat about moving to a better agency: establish exactly what you'd be working on. Even the best agencies have their less glamorous accounts, and if the job involves working exclusively on one of those, then perhaps it's not the opportunity you imagined. On the other hand, there is a school of thought that says that once you are in, you're in. There are plenty of people hired to do the "bread-and-butter" stuff who have gone on to produce work on the agency's showpiece accounts. Just make sure you know what you're getting into.

Another opportunity it may be worth moving for is the chance to creative direct. Some (not all) agencies find it hard to promote rank-and-file creatives to CD. They know their own creatives very well, so maybe aren't as excited by them as they are by a creative from another agency, who they don't know, so who might be somehow special, and thus more suitable to be a CD. So just as in all walks of life, sometimes you have to move to get a promotion.

LACK OF OPPORTUNITY

Sometimes *lack* of opportunity is a reason to move. If things aren't going well at your current agency—you haven't had much work out in a while, you're not getting the good briefs, or you don't think your ECD rates you—then you should have a look around and see if any better opportunities are out there.

FANCY A CHANGE?

Sometimes people move just because they fancy a change. It may be that you want to change cities, or even countries; one of the great things about our job is that you can do it anywhere. I have a friend who began his career in Sydney, and has since worked in Amsterdam, New York, London, and Los Angeles. And you don't necessarily need language skills to work abroad. If you speak English you can obviously work in countries such as the US, UK, Australia, South Africa, and New Zealand, but English is also near-universally spoken in the advertising industries of China, India, Singapore, and Holland. And if English is not your first language, that may not even matter, as long as your English is at least pretty good (copywriter) or passable (art director). It by no means needs to be perfect.

However, it's not necessary to move countries to have a change. Sometimes people just get bored of the accounts they're working on. This is especially true in agencies where creatives are assigned to specific accounts (common in the US). Even if you're working across every account in the building, you may find you see the same briefs come round again and again. You may want a change of scenery, to meet some different people, or just experience a different way of working.

There are no rules about the number of years you should stay at one agency. If you feel stale, move. On the other hand, if you're happy to come into work every day where you are, then don't shake things up.

HEADHUNTERS

The best way to move is via a headhunter.

As your career advances, it becomes more and more important to get to know the headhunters in your market. If you find one that you like, and trust, you can get excellent career advice from them. They will call you from time to time to discuss job opportunities. Tell them honestly what city you want to work in, what type of agency you want to work at, what type of accounts you would like to work on. The more you tell them, the more they can help you.

> *Make sure you have your salary story straight before you speak to a headhunter for the first time.*

They will be keen to establish what you are earning and what your expectations are, because that will help them determine the jobs you are suitable for.

A lot of creatives—because we're creative people not business people—don't feel comfortable with negotiation. The good news is that your headhunter will do the negotiating for you.

Headhunters may also ring you up and tell you that such-and-such a creative director is keen to meet you. If it's an interesting agency, meet them, even if you don't want to move right now. It's good to stick your nose out from time to time. If you don't like what you see, that's a good thing, because you'll be happier where you are. If you do like what you see, then it's a good thing, because now you have options.

THE INEXPLICABLE CURSE

Final word on this subject. After you move, be prepared for one of two things to happen. Occasionally a new team hits the ground running, cracks every brief in sight, and makes great ads right off the bat. But more often, there's an inexplicable curse, and it can take a new team *up to a year* to get an ad out. No one knows why this is. Maybe it's getting used to a new way of working, or a new culture. Whatever the reason, be aware of it—creative directors are, and they do make some allowances. So don't let that fear hold you back. If your reasons for moving are valid, move.

WORKING FREELANCE

Most creatives first start freelancing when they get fired from their permanent job, and don't want to go straight into another one. Others start out their careers freelancing, before settling into a permanent position later.

But to give you an overview, I'll set out some of the pros and cons of the freelance lifestyle here, and also Ten Tips on how to make it work.

PROS

The main plus is obvious: you can work when you want to (usually in the offices of the agency employing you but, in some cases, from home) and when you don't want to work, you don't have to.

This means you can take as many holidays as you want (albeit unpaid) and you're not limited to the two-weeks-at-a-time maximum that permanent employers impose. Many creatives combine freelance work with traveling, or take regular breaks to pursue personal projects.

"I've enjoyed having time to do other things, like writing novels and short films," says London freelancer Lorelei Mathias. "And being freelance gives you a chance to play the field a bit before settling down in the perfect job."

"Freelance definitely broadens your outlook," agrees experienced UK freelancer Nathalie Turton. "You get to see how different agencies all do things so differently. Through my years of freelance I have been offered permanent jobs but I haven't wanted to give up freelancing."

"You're always on your toes," she adds, "which keeps things exciting. Every week/month it's a different journey to work, a different office, different people, different briefs."

For many, a further attraction is that you're not involved in agency politics, and not required to take on much responsibility.

Most of all, when you're working, the money is excellent (freelancers are paid a much higher daily rate than regular staff, to compensate them for the short-term nature of the contract).

And you may occasionally get a job where you're brought in for an emergency…then no one briefs you for a month, so you're getting money for nothing. As well as being able to earn a higher income, you actually pay a lot less tax, because freelancers are allowed to offset a whole slew of expenses.

"Assuming that you are temperamentally suited and have a decent work ethic, freelancing can be a great way to go," says Jim Morris, a US freelancer who goes by the brand-name "The Communicaterer." "But you won't know for sure unless you give it a try. Some people thrive on the autonomy, flexibility, and liberating work-lifestyle that freelancing can offer. Others are so uncomfortable with not knowing when the next assignment will come that they become chronically anxious."

CONS

Insecurity. As soon as you get one job, you have to organize the next one. You're constantly on the lookout for work.

And aside from the challenges of the lifestyle that you'll have to come to terms with in your mind, there may be challenges to face in terms of how you're treated in your agency.

Some places will look after you well, setting you up with IT the day you arrive, and giving you good assignments. Perhaps their attitude is they're paying you twice as much as the permanent staffers, so they might as well get their money's worth.

But in some agencies you'll get treated like a dog—the worst briefs, and account handlers and planners constantly rewriting your work because they don't know you and have no incentive to build a relationship with you.

And while ostensibly you are paid quite well, actually getting the money can be a problem. There seems to be a perception in some agencies that freelancers do not need to eat, pay their mortgages or buy pants, thus no need to pay their invoice.

Some freelancers report that they don't actually give you money until you threaten to firebomb the finance department. And even then they don't pay you; they just don the asbestos suits they keep under their desks. Plus, they automatically lose your first invoice.

The social side of being a freelancer can be less fulfilling than being on-staff. Freelancers are like novice fighter pilots, i.e. there is a perception that you're not going to be around for long, so in some agencies people don't bother getting to know you…or even acknowledge you in the corridor.

"You feel like the New Person all the time, and that can be draining," says Lorelei Mathias. "You don't know what to talk about when you bump into strangers in the lift."

There often isn't enough help too. It is assumed that freelancers are unlike normal people and will automatically know where the printer is. Even then, it may take IT three days to attach you to that printer. Perhaps they assume that freelancers are unlike everyone else and don't need to print anything.

(Bringing in your own laptop may help, though it may be impossible to get it to attach to the agency's network. Even though three IT guys are at your desk staring at it and saying "server" a lot. They will, however, admire it because, for tax reasons, you will have bought a really nice one.)

"We once worked at an agency for a whole month without access to a printer or the internet," reports one freelancer, who prefers to remain anonymous. "Luckily I had my own laptop, otherwise I wouldn't have had a computer either. And every Friday they'd all go to the pub and 'forget' to invite us. It was like being bullied at school."

The briefs you will be given are often the most difficult ones in the agency. They will have been attempted, multiple times, over an entire year, by every creative/planner/desperate account man in the building, and remain resolutely uncracked. The creative director will have given up on them and you will be reviewing with the head of planning, who by this stage has been driven quite mad by the project. You will be informed that the client will leave the agency if you don't crack the brief in the next three days.

(This is understandable in a way. The role of a freelancer is to pick up the slack, work that's going spare, and the really great briefs are rarely going spare.)

You may find that when you turn up for work on your first day, the person who got you in will have carefully omitted to tell anyone about your impending arrival. He will also be out at a meeting all morning so that you will have lost an entire half-day of the three you have been allotted to crack this uncrackable brief.

No one will tell you about the security system and you will get trapped in a stairwell. For some reason people assume freelancers are different from normal people and they have already received their security passes by magic or something.

For some, it's frustrating that you rarely get to see any projects through to fruition. That means no shoots, no nice lunches while in edits, and little produced work for your book.

"As great as freelancing is, you need to be permanent somewhere in order to get work out, and move up the career ladder," advises Nathalie Turton. "As a freelancer you kind of move horizontally." The bottom line is that if you have a really good book...you will be in high demand, get a lot of money, and good briefs. The second tier of freelancers might also make decent money—but won't get briefs good enough to improve their book.

The better your book, the better your freelance gig. Moral: if you fancy the freelance life, delay starting until you have some really good work in your book. Then you can live that life well.

TEN TIPS FOR SUCCESSFUL FREELANCING

1   <u>Get an accountant.</u> Life is far too short for toiling over Excel grids.

2   <u>Network.</u> Even if you're relatively inexperienced, you have a more extensive network than you realize. Your network consists of everyone you know, even slightly. Make frequent contact with all these people and let it be known you are available, champing at the bit.

3   <u>Go to agencies' creative services people directly.</u> Although headhunters are very useful, you can't rely on them alone. And many agencies like being able to book a team directly, rather than pay headhunters' fees.

4   <u>Get a portable hard drive and save your work on it as you go.</u> Better than chasing it up once you've left.

5   <u>Err on the side of charging more than you're comfortable with.</u> Successful freelancers charge whatever the market will bear. The higher rate or fee you can establish for yourself, the more perceived value you will have.
    "Freelancers, especially early on, tend to price their services timidly, insecurely," reckons Jim Morris. "They don't know their market value and are afraid of being shut out of a project by overpricing themselves. Learn what the hourly rate and day rate range is for lightweights through heavyweights in your field. If you come in a little high, the client will usually let you know, giving you an opportunity to reduce your rate or fee. These matters are usually negotiable, so negotiate."

6   <u>Do take holidays</u>—and enjoy the fact that you can go for longer than two weeks if you want. Although…be aware of the "cigarette and bus" rule. The moment you book a holiday, someone will call offering you work.

7   <u>In between jobs, make the most of your time.</u> Don't just sit around panicking, but use that time to pursue other creative projects outside the advertising bubble. Make short films, write articles, get out that novel you have inside you.

8   Organization and creativity are rarely friends, but if you're becoming freelance you'll need to get yourself somewhat organized. <u>Invoice regularly and be prepared to become a "chaser."</u>

9   <u>Market yourself.</u> The more top-of-mind with the more prospective clients you can be, the greater are your chances of landing a freelance gig. It may sound old-school, but a mailer, with a simple, interesting visual or bit of language, can be very effective. Whatever marketing tack you take, be sure it doesn't entail too much work, or else you won't be able to sustain the effort.

10 Money. <u>Make sure you have some in the bank.</u> As discussed, some places take three months to pay you. And get a second bank account, in which to stash a portion of your earnings away for your tax bill, when it comes.

WHAT TO DO WHEN YOU GET FIRED

Sh*t-canned. Made redundant. Laid off. The sack. Given your cards. Given your marching orders. Kicked out.

Like anything naughty, dirty, or embarrassing—think of booze, cash, and boobs—getting the boot has many synonyms.

No statistics specific to our industry are available, but anecdotal evidence suggests that you are almost certain to be fired at some point. Ours is a notoriously insecure business.

But some argue that getting fired from time to time is actually healthy.

Kash Sree, the talented UK-born creative behind Nike "Tag," has said in interviews that "if you're not doing at least one thing every year that could get you fired, you're not pushing hard enough."

So when is it most likely to happen? You're probably in most danger at the beginning of your career, before you're established. The middle bit is tricky too, when you're earning a reasonable salary but don't yet have a huge reputation. And senior creatives certainly aren't immune. Some get to a point where they think they can't be fired, because they're integral to some large account or other. However, the relationship with the creatives is never as important to clients as the relationship with the suits. And the life expectancy of the creative director himself is notoriously short, as he's the easiest person to blame when the agency's work (like 99 percent of all ad agencies) falls short of the industry's Top 1 percent.

Occasionally, being fired can be a positive. I know of one team that had decided to leave their agency, and they got another job, but before they could resign, the ECD dropped by to say he was letting them go. They started work at their new agency on Monday, with three months' money in their pockets.

But usually it isn't.

BLAME

I have been fired twice in my career.

The first time it happened, I was working at Saatchi & Saatchi in London when Maurice and his brother Charles quit the agency to set up their own firm—M&C Saatchi. They took about one-third of the clients with them. Obviously, redundancies had to be made. I was working on my own, because I had recently split up with my art director. I had also fallen out with my boss (long story). I was a junior creative—only two years' experience—and while I had produced a few ads here and there, I hadn't done anything particularly brilliant. So in a nutshell, given that they had to get rid of about 15 creatives, I could hardly blame them for getting rid of me, and I could hardly blame myself either. Could I?

The second time, I was working at a really bad small agency, when the two founding partners decided to separate, the company was broken up, and there was no job any more for my partner and me. Once again, I told myself it was not my fault.

Getting fired is a traumatic experience that can badly dent your confidence. It was several years before I could walk down Charlotte Street, past the Saatchi's building, because it was too upsetting and I was afraid I might run into someone I knew.

And it's that trauma, I believe, that leads people to construct elaborate theories as to how undeserving and unlucky they were to get fired, how blameless. It's a sensible strategy. The last thing your ego needs in times of crisis is to start questioning itself. That's why most people who are fired get mad at their boss. And they get mad at the company—after all, it's a ridiculous agency, which started going downhill years ago.

It took me years to realize that the person responsible for my firings was me.

In the Saatchi's case, it's true that they would never have had to make redundancies if the M&C split hadn't happened. And I was a singleton. But the fact is, they chose to fire me, and keep others.

In the case of the small agency, it was even more clear-cut. This shop split into two even tinier agencies, neither of which wanted me (or my partner). The only other creative working there at the time *did* get taken on by one of the new units...but I didn't.

So at the risk of sounding like one of those self-help books with titles like *"He's Just Not That Into You"* or *"Yes You Do Have A Fat Bum"*…what I'm saying is that if you do get fired, it is your fault.

In letting people go, an agency will always choose the people it thinks are least good value for money, the least talented, the least fun to have around, the least suited to the agency's culture, and the most easily replaceable.

The first of these, in this advanced stage of capitalism that we inhabit, is by far the most important. The quality of work you produce relative to the dollars that you cost—that's the most important thing they look at.

The reason I'm being so brutal is that I believe the sooner you can figure out where you've gone wrong, the sooner you can start to put things right.

Yes, by all means go through a phase of blaming your boss, your partner, or the idiot clients who failed to buy your best ideas. But after that, you must enter a period of introspection.

ARE YOU HAPPY WITH YOUR WORK?

The best piece of advice I was given when I got fired was by Richard Myers, former European creative director at Saatchi's. He said to me: *"Are you happy with the work you have in your book? That's the only thing that matters."*

I took a look at my book and realized I wasn't happy with my work. It was OK, but it wasn't the best I could do. Truth was, I had been having an enormous amount of fun in my first job—too much, really, like coming in to work at 11am and playing football in the corridor—but I hadn't done great work. The decision I made was to take my job more seriously and, while still having fun, not goof around quite so much.

If you were already doing the best work you can—and it seems that wasn't good enough—or you have commitments that prevent you putting more time and effort in, or you just don't *want* to put that much time and effort into a job, then you can simply drop down a notch or two in the food chain for your next position—that's a perfectly valid call to make too.

QUESTIONS TO ASK YOURSELF

Are you with the right partner? Were you working hard enough? Were you working smart enough? Were you too feisty, or too compliant? Were you working somewhere you didn't fit in? Had you taken on too much responsibility or, conversely, not enough? Were you working somewhere they don't like the type of work you do? Would you be better suited to a specialist agency of some kind? If you were working above-the-line, would you be better suited to a job below-the-line, or vice versa? Were you in the right city, the right country? Was there something in your home life or your personal life that stopped you from succeeding?

Figure out what the problem was, and fix it.

CHAPTER 8
THE INTANGIBLE ASPECTS OF SUCCESS

PERSISTENCE

The temptation to stop is always strong.

Yes! Got something—hurrah! Now we can check our e-mails and surf the internet.

Don't.

Look, I know the feeling, believe me. Thinking is maybe the hardest work there is, aside from digging a trench. And as soon as you have something that works, the desire to down tools is overwhelming.

So you find yourself ignoring the little voice in your head. The voice that says *"It's a bit like that other ad from last year"* or *"It works, but it's only OK."*

Do not ignore that voice. If you know in your heart of hearts there's a problem with the idea, it's pretty certain your creative director will agree with you.

Learn to recognize the "false friends"—the ideas that *seem* strong enough to have cracked the problem, but that aren't.

One of the most common false friends is the brilliant one-off ad. In creative-showcase magazines like *Luerzer's Archive* you will often see a one-off ad shot in three different ways, claiming to be a campaign. It isn't.

Another false friend is the campaign that consists of one great ad, one ad that's not too bad, and no third one. Sadly, when this is the case, you haven't really got a campaign. The only solution if a genuine campaign is required is to think of something else.

Another is the kind of idea that will translate into a good ad only if the execution is perfect. Once again, you must turn that chap away. Why? Because your idea has to be 120 percent.

I learned this term from Andrew Fraser (formerly a CD at DDB London) when I showed him an idea for a print ad and his reaction was *"Yes, it's fine, it works,"* but his tone of voice told me he wasn't buying it. I asked what the problem was. He replied:

> *"Your idea has to be 120 percent, to survive the weakening."*

Here is a diagram of what I think he meant.

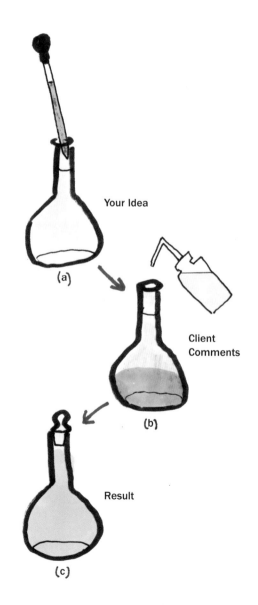

Your Idea

(a)

Client Comments

(b)

Result

(c)

If you're out of ideas on the brief you're working on, try working on a different one. Many creatives find it's actually helpful to have two or three briefs on the go at once. You work on something for an hour, and then switch. That way you don't hit brick walls.

Good creatives never dry up.

It's common that your first proposal gets blown out by the client—at this point, many teams quit. They feel they've already cracked the brief once…perhaps they don't believe they can crack it again. Or they don't want to. Or they're now angry. But good creatives go back to the same coal-face, to the same tunnel that just blew up in their faces, find another seam, and start mining it.

Even if another route has been bought by the creative director, or even approved by the client, the really exceptional creatives don't quit. Some teams are so bloody-minded they never stop working on a brief until the ad appears on air. And why not? There are so many occasions when an ad is about to go into production but gets killed, just before it was due to be born. That's when you can step in.

It's a cliché of creative problem-solving that your best idea is always your first one or your last one. What this means is, sometimes you just find you have the answer straight away. And when you don't, you're in for a long struggle. Incidentally, I'm a big fan of the first thought. There's something pure and visceral about your instant response to a brief that sets it apart from solutions you've strived over. Never discount your first thought, however insane it may appear. And if you really feel that it's cracked the brief, don't waste your time carrying on—put your time into something else. On the other hand, be honest with yourself. If your first thought has not delivered the answer, you're going to need to carry on.

Though it may seem painful, keeping going is the right thing to do. As someone once said, the way to have a good idea is to have a lot of them.

You will have to stop eventually, for sure. But not yet.

KEEP LEARNING

When you're a junior in a sound suite/editing suite/retouching studio it's easy to feel overawed, because everyone else in the room knows what they're doing, and you may not have a clue.

I highly recommend you to ask. Not easy, because that means admitting your ignorance, and nobody likes to look dumb.

But if you don't ask questions, you don't extend your knowledge.

Once you get used to the embarrassment, it's fine. And it's good to get used to it, because you'll need to keep asking questions throughout your career.

Everyone knows that Darwin defined evolution in terms of the survival of the fittest, but what's less well understood is that "fittest" doesn't mean smartest or strongest; it means most adaptable.

So to have a successful career in advertising, or indeed any field, you have to keep learning. It's a big mistake to start off your career by learning, and then as soon as you've had some success, rest on your laurels. Our industry changes too quickly for that. There are constant advances in technology, which push back the boundaries of what's achievable.

Alexandre Gama, president and chief creative officer, Neogama BBH (Brazil) says that;

"All creatives should play Nintendo Wii—any game, once a week, or at weekends. There's no better lesson in interactivity. If the Wii is not your ballgame, try Xbox 360 or PlayStation 3. But you have to play it in order to really understand what kind of world we're living in today. Action, visuals, animation, soundtrack, plots. And, of course, fun. OK, reading good books, going to art shows, and watching movies is seriously important as they are the foundation of cultural background and fundamental in building a solid creative repertoire. But do play a little Wii once in a while."

Keep meeting people who know things you don't, and be happy to look stupid in front of them.

Do courses. Every agency has a training budget they need to spend—make sure some of it goes your way. Take the obvious courses like presentation skills and radio production, but take some non-obvious ones too. It may not be immediately apparent how screenwriting, poetry, printmaking, or life drawing can help your advertising career. But they can.

Sure, it's unlikely these activities will give you a solution to the brief you're currently working on. But you need to keep filling the well—the part of your unconscious that is teeming with interesting ideas and images—the place you draw your ideas from.

Having to come up with ideas every day is most draining. Keep the flow of new ones coming in; otherwise one day you'll go to the well and it'll be empty.

Keep doing things you haven't done before, talk to people who other people never talk to, and look at weird sh*t.

John Webster used to regularly visit a local greetings card store and spend five minutes flipping through the cards. Why? For the quick hit of jokes, images, and surreal little nothings. Websites are the modern equivalent—look at a wide range, daily.

I'm not talking about finding ideas to rip off. I'm talking about keeping your mind open, alive, and unconventional.

That's what you need to do on an ongoing basis to stay creative, and employable, throughout your career.

CHALLENGE YOURSELF

Also, challenge yourself. Most people prefer to spend time doing things they already know how to, and are good at. But if you only do what you already know, you'll quickly become stale. And getting stale is the biggest risk to your career.

Keep yourself fresh by taking on projects you *don't* know how to do. Yes, they can go wrong. But it's so much more fun.

If going to work feels like settling into a warm bath, you need to shake something up. Consider moving agencies, or changing partners.

Just for clarity, I'm not recommending a life of constant discomfort. All I'm saying is that creativity requires stimulation, and lack of stimulation will lead you gently to the armchair of complacency.

Avoid that armchair.

*Examples of the type of weird sh*t you should regularly be looking at. In this case, from the website www.VVork.com.*

SOCIALIZING

Years ago there was a group of London ad-men who called themselves the 11.01 Club—named after the time they arrived at the pub every morning.

The US series *Mad Men*, as well as being superbly well plotted and entertaining, has amazed audiences with its depiction of 1960s ad agency staff drinking whisky in their offices, having sex in their offices, and smoking *everywhere*.

Those days are long gone.

The business has even become more serious in the few years since I have been in it. E-mail, Blackberries, and electronic diaries have a lot to answer for.

Nevertheless, it's still a fun business compared to a job in accountancy, so you'd be missing out if you didn't make the most of the fun available. Ad people are incapable of finishing a big project without having a celebratory lunch, and there are many, many nights out in a year—from leaving do's to agency parties to awards do's.

But this isn't a book about how to have fun. It's about how to be successful, and there is undoubtedly an aspect to socializing that can further your career.

In *Ogilvy on Advertising*, David Ogilvy advised agency managers to "*Get rid of sad dogs who spread gloom.*" Now, I'm fairly certain he was referring more to account handlers than creatives. If you're a grouchy depressive who can only make eye contact with another person's shoes you will still be fine, if you're a creative whose work is good. But it's not an approach that will actively boost your career.

And, conversely, being considered a "cultural asset" in an agency is nowhere near as important as doing good work. But, it never hurt anyone.

The fact is that people who know you and like you will be more inclined to help you, whether that be giving you a job or just a piece of useful advice.

Please note that I'm not advising any kind of calculated and cold-hearted networking strategy. Far from it. In fact, anyone who tries too hard to ingratiate themselves is quite rightly shunned. All I am suggesting is if you do go out to an agency or industry event, that you have fun, be yourself, and *talk to people*. That way, as well as having a good time, you'll be helping yourself career-wise.

I've lost count of the number of casual chats I've had in the agency pub in which I've learned useful stuff from planners and account handlers—like which briefs are about to come up, what a client "really" thinks about an ad we've presented, or who is about to be fired.

It's even more essential to socialize with your fellow creatives. First of all, there's no one better to whinge to. And although none of you would think of an after-work drink as an information-sharing session, you do learn a lot from your colleagues. With your closest friends, you'll even end up sharing how much each of you is earning, and ideas on how to ask the boss for more.

INDUSTRY EVENTS

At industry events like awards do's, you meet folk from other agencies. Ad people make for a lively crowd, and these events can be some of the best nights out of the year.

> *As well as making new friends, you get the chance to swap information about each other's agencies.*

There's nothing like hearing from the horse's mouth exactly what a place is like to work at. You'll also discuss what you've been working on, and from that conversation you'll learn about which directors they rate, which photographers, and maybe hear opinions on what makes for good advertising that could vary enormously from what you're used to hearing in your own agency.

And then there's Cannes.

If you get the chance to go to the advertising festival at Cannes, go. There is much about Cannes that is very, very wrong. But it's so much fun.

Expect to find yourself crashing pool parties at villas in the hills; talking total sh*t in the Gutter Bar at 4am; and stumbling around the Croisette at dawn trying to remember what street the ludicrously overpriced Hotel Bedbug is on.

But be aware of the unwritten rules of Cannes and other industry events. You're allowed to behave badly —and with free booze and nightclubs it's quite hard not to—but you're not allowed to be an idiot. It's not cool to be so drunk that you throw up in your MD's handbag. And it's not endearing to be lecherous.

So the summary on socializing is "do what comes naturally." You'll make friends and learn vital information. And if you're a fun guy who people like, that won't harm your career at all.

RAISING YOUR PROFILE

If you keep quiet, the world won't notice you.

One of the biggest sources of amazement to me is how appallingly bad most creatives are at marketing themselves. We spend our whole working lives getting attention for the brands we work on, generating PR for them, and communicating their benefits to people. And then what do we do to PR ourselves? Nothing.

> *The ability to promote yourself is an advantage in every field of human activity.*

For example, it's said that Tesla was a much better inventor than Edison...but Edison had better PR.

GETTING TALKED ABOUT

Let's look at a couple of examples of people in our industry who understand the value of a good profile.

Siimon Reynolds (interviewed in this book) is arguably Australia's most successful ad-man. Did adding the extra "i" to his name help him to become a creative director? Probably not. Did writing books like *365 Ways to Live to 100* and *Become Happy in 8 Minutes* help him start his own agency? Probably not. Did a regular spot on the Australian version of the *Dragons' Den* TV show help him found one of Australia's largest communications groups, which today employs over 6,000 people? Probably not, but you can see where I'm going with this. Everything Siimon Reynolds does signals that he's an unusual, interesting, and creative individual, and it gets him talked about.

In the UK, we have Graham Fink, ECD of M&C Saatchi, and one of the most talented creatives Britain has ever produced. But he also knows how to sell himself. He once turned up to the British Television Advertising Awards dressed as Robin Hood, complete with a bow but no arrows, saying he hoped to fill his quiver at the ceremony (the BTAA award is an arrow). He didn't actually win any arrows that night, but the next day, who do you think everyone was talking about?

In recent times, two of the most effective PR men in our business have been French creative duo Fred & Farid, now running their own agency in Paris.

Here are my five favorite Fred & Farid stories. (N.B. These may not all be true... but they are stories people tell—and they all add to the F&F myth.)

1 In an interview, they once claimed they lived in the same apartment, went to the same films, and ate exactly the same food as each other every day, so they could "think as one."
2 They once stuffed an account man into a bin.
3 They once walked into a creative's office, shut the door, told him: "Your work, it is sh*t," and walked out again.
4 They once pushed everyone's desks against the wall to clear a space so they could practise kickboxing—in the middle of the creative department.
5 They once halted a commercial shoot so they could be interviewed by *Shots* magazine.

Some might write off such antics as "stunts." Maybe they are. But if a stunt is fun enough and clever enough, then it doesn't feel gratuitous, it doesn't backfire, and it successfully builds profile.

Nevertheless, these are extreme examples, and not ones everyone could follow. Adam Ant sang *"ridicule is nothing to be scared of,"* but not everyone likes to risk it. Unless you are extremely thick-skinned, flamboyant, and attention-craving—basically, a show-off—I don't recommend the above tactics. However, it's worth bearing in mind the lengths that some people are prepared to go to, to get noticed. And you're competing with them.

There are a few quieter types who prefer to let their work speak for itself. But not many, especially among ECDs. Someone who reaches the level of ECD—someone talented enough to command a huge salary and dictate the destiny of an entire company—is likely to be a remarkable person, and remarkable people naturally attract attention because they're, well, remarkable in some way. They have to be.

At the top level, doing great work is not enough.

An agency ECD is the "figurehead" of the company—a charismatic figure, able to attract top creative talent, and clients.

MAKING YOUR NAME

So how do you make a name for yourself?

As a junior, you should be sending your work out to the creative magazines (e.g. *Archive, Creative Review*) and to ad blogs. As a middleweight, you should be comfortable speaking to journalists about your work (assuming your employer allows this—some don't let staffers other than management speak to the trade press). And as a senior creative you should be actively thinking of ways to build your personal profile. Ways to do this include putting yourself forward for election to industry bodies, speaking at industry events, and writing articles for the trade press and online publications, or finding a way to have them interview you.

The benefits of a profile should be obvious. Just as people prefer to buy brands they have heard of, they prefer to hire people they have heard of. If an ECD is hiring, he will be more likely to give an interview to a team that he has heard of because they were in *Campaign* last week than a team he has never heard of. And if an agency CEO is looking for a new ECD, he is more likely to hire the person with a massive industry profile, someone whose career is followed by the trade press and whose next move is eagerly anticipated, rather than someone whose hiring will prompt the dreaded question *"Who?"*

Please don't think I'm saying it's less important to be talented than to have good PR. That isn't the case. In fact, it's naïve to think that anyone could reach the top without talent, since even the most shameless self-promoters need some success to promote. Some might stretch their triumphs thin—in other words, they might do one or two good ads, and through self-promotion gain a high position and maintain it without doing any good work again. But not many. Our business is too lean and ruthless nowadays for people to do well if they're not performing, however well known they've become.

LOOK CREATIVE

Are you one of those people who thinks it doesn't matter what you wear in life—all that matters is what you do, and what you say?

If so…what would you think of a college professor who lectured in a bikini?

Gotcha.

What you wear may seem trivial, but is actually important.

Whenever I raise this topic, I get a defensive reaction. People have an ingrained belief that clothes are a silly thing to care about, and they are quick to slap me down and tell me "No one gives a stuff what you wear." But that's not correct.

American anthropologist Ray Birdwhistell estimated the non-verbal at 65 percent of all communication received. And a big part of what you communicate non-verbally comes from what you wear—your clothes send signals.

There are very good reasons why the riot police don't wear pink.

Surely we creatives—we who earn our living creating images—should know better than to dismiss the importance of "look."

We're experts at presenting brands in the best possible light. So why do we never consider how we're presenting ourselves? How come a creative understands that it's worth spending hours retouching a photo of a yogurt pot, because he knows that the tiniest tweaks to the visual styling of this milk-based dessert will affect how the consumer perceives it…and yet refuses to even contemplate that his own appearance affects how he is perceived?

Our business is subjective, and your success (or failure) will depend considerably on your perception-management skills. And what you wear forms part of how you're perceived. No one knows for sure if an idea that you present to them is any good or not. The main thing that will convince them is you telling them it is. And if you look like a person who has good ideas, then that will make a difference.

After grudgingly accepting that what they wear is a form of communication, people sometimes protest I'm advising "dress wacky." I'm not. Absolutely not. Unless you want to be perceived as wacky? Like anyone trying too hard, the creative trying desperately to look creative is an embarrassment. And just as the *least* creative agencies often have the funkiest décor, there's a slight suspicion that less creative people feel a greater need to look cutting-edge. They're following the rule of "If you can't *be* creative, you might as well look creative."

A US creative observes: "Go to the worst agencies and you'll see the creative department dressed in the trendiest togs with painstakingly funky hairdos and $800 boots. Lots of tattoos also. Whereas at the places doing good work, the clothing is pretty secondary, leaning heavily towards the collegiate and comfortable."

THE "CREATIVE UNIFORM"?

The final objection I hear is that I'm suggesting people adopt some kind of "creative uniform." (Just as there's a uniform for lawyers, postmen, and off-duty footballers, there's a uniform for creative people too. I won't attempt to describe this, since it varies country by country and city by city, and will be out of date by the time you read this. But a quick stroll through any advertising agency creative department, record label, or TV production company should be enough to convince you it exists.)

Those who wear the "creative uniform" do so because it sends out a strong non-verbal signal: "I'm part of the group." I'm not suggesting you have to go out and buy this uniform; it's up to you whether you want to send that message or not. Perhaps you want to send the opposite signal: Paul Arden, the great Saatchi's CD, for example, often dressed like a country gentleman. In a world of wannabe urban hipsters, he stood out a mile. But at least be aware of what signal you are sending.

There's a wide variety of styles among those who look creative, according to what type of creativity they consciously or unconsciously want to project. Here are some examples:

"Writer" with a capital W: wear this kind of gear and no one will ever rework your headlines. And they will automatically think the dialogue in your TV commercials is brilliant.

Trendy: this look says *"I know what's hot right now."* How can an account team question your choice of music track for a commercial, when you look like this?

Arty: become unassailable on all matters relating to typography and design.

OK, so these descriptions are a little tongue-in-cheek, but I hope they expand my point—what you wear not only influences whether people think you're good or not, it even tells them which *aspects* of the job you're good at. Powerful stuff.

Just to be ultra-clear, I'm not proposing that you adopt one of these uniforms, or indeed any uniform. Wear what you want. Be yourself.

> *But be aware of the messages that your clothes are sending, and dress in accordance with what you want to say.*

For example, if you're looking to get promoted to creative director, it may be time to purchase a jacket.

How you look does make a difference. Make it make a difference in your favor.

DON'T BEHAVE

In no way do I condone "bad" behavior from creatives, like turning up late for meetings, being rude to people, not listening, or being untidy. All of that is not on.

What I am advocating when I say *"Don't behave"* is—don't do things just because that's the way they're always done, or to make things easier for other people, at the expense of the work.

Here are some examples to explain what I'm talking about:

Behaving means spending 90 percent of your day on that retail radio brief you've been given, with almost no time left over for the big TV brief that's floating around the department. Mistake. Spend no more than 50 percent of your time doing what you're supposed to do, and the other 50 percent on stuff that can actually move your career forward.

Behaving means saying yes when the account team ask you to write an alternative ("safe") version of your script, which they promise they will only present to the client as a fall-back. Doing this is certainly easier and nicer, since refusing to do it will cause an argument. But sometimes you have to be willing to have disagreements. Be polite, but be firm, and explain that you're not doing it, because you don't think it's the right thing to do, and why.

Behaving means only coming back with ideas that are on brief, and for the media specified on the brief. A lot of creatives don't want to "cause a problem" by presenting, say, a proposal for a TV documentary when the brief asked for a press ad. Or an idea about "excitement" when the brief requested "reliability." If you've got a great idea, people will fight to make it happen. If you have an average idea, no one will remember that you came up with something on brief, on time, and for the right medium. They actually won't remember it at all. Bill Bernbach said: "*I don't want people who do the right things. I want people who do inspiring things.*"

Behaving means agreeing with your creative director, even when you think he's wrong and is going to mess up the ad. Young creatives normally find it impossible to get CDs to change their minds about anything. So after an initial rebellious period, lasting anything between two weeks and two years, they become compliant. This is a mistake. No human being is right all the time. Of course, when you've only just started, your CD is far more likely to be right than you are. But what if he isn't? Tell him how you'd do it. Be civil, and give him your reasons. You probably still won't change his mind, since most CDs are unbelievably egotistical, but if you say nothing, you're certain not to get your way. (N.B. If he still disagrees, don't persist indefinitely. Someone has to make the call, and the agency has asked him to do that, not you.)

Behaving means doing an average job on a dull brief for a difficult client, a.k.a. *"You're really helping us out here."* I've seen countless teams suckered into "taking one for the team" on a dull bit of business. Before they know it, they are the go-to guys for *all* dull bits of business. Then the current creative director gets fired, a new one comes in...and fires that team, because all they have produced is mediocre work for the last three years—despite keeping the client happy and the money rolling in. The thanks you get for behaving in the long run? The bullet.

In short, don't behave. It won't get you anywhere. And it's not fun.

The main difficulty comes when you are given a straight-out order to work on a dull brief.

In *Bartleby*, an 1853 novella by Herman Melville, the titular character—who works as a clerk in a law firm—simply responds to any requests to perform work duties with the phrase *"I would prefer not to."* But this existentialist mode of resistance doesn't end well for Bartleby. And while a senior or high-profile creative might be able to turn down an unappetizing project, most creatives have to take whatever briefs they're given.

THREE APPROACHES TO A DULL BRIEF

1   The first, which is the approach I most recommend, is to execute this brief as quickly as possible, leaving you time to work on other things as well.
2   The second, which is difficult and time-consuming, but potentially rewarding, is to try to do something good on every brief. Some agencies have been able to do great work on hitherto uncreative accounts, e.g. Crispin Porter for Burger King, and Saatchi & Saatchi NY for Tide. And some creatives actively enjoy a challenge.
       I once asked Mark Waites, a creative director and co-founder of Mother, how his agency managed to do such good work for even the most difficult clients. "It's simple," he told me. "Just never show them a bad ad." He was being disingenuous though. Be warned that if you choose to follow this route, it is not simple. In fact it's bloody hard work.
3   The third and final approach is one I call "playing to lose." This is a method of avoiding bad briefs. But it has to be done cleverly. For the good of your reputation, you can't do it in a way that makes you look difficult, arrogant, or prima-donna-ish.

Years ago, when I worked at Saatchi's, some friends of mine—a talented team—got briefed on Oil of Olay.

They came back with a script about a woman who is dead. However, because her friends regularly apply Oil of Olay to her face, no one realizes. (The idea was based on the movie *Weekend At Bernie's*.)

This was a fun and lateral way to demonstrate what the product does for your skin, but of course, not something that Procter & Gamble could ever buy.

K**** and C***** were never given a P&G brief again. And yet, no one could say they hadn't tried, or hadn't done a good job. That is playing to lose. It's an advanced skill, and a high-risk strategy, but nevertheless, one you may wish occasionally to deploy.

AGENCY LIFE

Some agencies are more sociable than others, but in general, it's still an industry that drinks more than it should, and is constantly celebrating someone's arrival, departure, or birthday.

People who have left advertising often say that what they most miss is the banter. And although deadlines are getting shorter and staffing levels tighter, there's still plenty of chat to be had.

Because it's an industry that's short on facts and long on opinions, it does tend to attract the confident. In fact, if you don't state your opinions confidently, you won't last. You have more chance of selling an average idea if you are confident than a brilliant idea if you are not. Unfair, but that's how it works. If you're not confident, you'll either have to fake it, or work on it.

The flipside of confidence is arrogance. Never become arrogant, however many times you're proved right. And avoid vanity. Of course it's fine to be well dressed and well groomed. But it's better to be a person of substance and integrity. Actually, why make a choice here? Be both.

Agency décor is sometimes painfully "creative," but is usually at least modern. It could be a lot worse. You could be working in a bank. Or a coal mine. Just make sure your office environment is suitable for working. Open-plan is a curse, caused by interior designers who think advertising people want somewhere "buzzy." But to be creative, you need uninterrupted thinking time. Many creatives end up doing their creative thinking at home, on public transportation, or in cafés…and the office becomes just a place for meetings and e-mails. If you're finding it difficult to think in the office, don't hesitate to pop out for a bit. No one will miss you. And if they do, so what? Better to have people thinking that you bunk off a lot, than that you never have any ideas.

Office decoration is quite an art. My partner and I put up posters of ads that we're proud of, scamps of ads we've written but that haven't been made yet, funny notes people have left us, and images we find beautiful or amusing. Some creatives put "stimulating" pictures on their walls. I personally don't see how this can make any difference, since after a day or so, anything you put on your wall becomes invisible to you, it just fades into the background. Nevertheless, these items do have a function—as a signalling system to visitors, telling them what kind of people you are, and what you find important or interesting.

Watch your internet consumption. Too little and you will come across as an idiot. Too much, ditto.

OFFICE DATING

Spending so much time in the office can leave little time for a personal life. Maybe that's why so many people in advertising combine the two. They socialize with the people they work with, and vice versa. Inevitably, they end up dating them, despite the old advice not to dip your pen in company ink.

It happens in every profession: lawyers date other lawyers, doctors date other doctors. But there's a perception that advertising is more incestuous than most—perhaps because with so many industry parties and events, there are simply more opportunities to, ahem, get to know your co-workers.

Of course, every relationship that ends, ends badly.

One of you is going to feel aggrieved. One of you is going to be portrayed as the guilty party. After you break up, the situation can become awkward. So if you're the sort of person who doesn't like awkward situations, don't date someone in your own agency.

In a bigger agency it isn't so bad, because chances are you won't see them that often. But in a small agency, a ruined relationship can poison the entire atmosphere. One of you may have to leave.

Some people in advertising prefer to date civilians— they find it reassuring that their partner won't care if the client changes the copy yet again. Others prefer to go out with someone who understands what they do, and can feel their pain.

YOUR PERSONAL LIFE

It would be utterly ridiculous of me to give you advice on how to live your life. So I won't.

And if anyone else tries to—don't listen.

There is quite simply no right or wrong way for a creative person to live.

Flaubert famously advised: *"Be regular and orderly in your life…so that you may be violent and original in your work."*

Jack Kerouac said: "The only people for me are the mad ones, the ones who are mad to live, mad to talk, mad to be saved, desirous of everything at the same time, the ones who never yawn or say a commonplace thing, but burn, burn, burn, like fabulous yellow roman candles exploding like spiders across the stars and in the middle you see the blue centerlight pop and everybody goes 'Awww!'"

Or to put it another way—Jimi Hendrix took drugs for breakfast, Van Morrison is teetotal. But both count as pretty creative.

So whatever you're doing, don't think it's wrong. Just make sure you're doing what's right for you. If you're an urban outlaw, don't go to stay at your grandmother's house in a nice, neat suburb "to save money." You won't be happy. And if you're the kind of person who enjoys gardening and drinking cups of tea at the weekend, don't worry that you "really" should be at an anarchist festival.

Some people spend their weekends at work. That's OK too.

For some, advertising is a vocation—they always knew they wanted to go into advertising, just as others knew they would be a priest, or a doctor. This type of person knows which ads each director has shot, can name every current campaign for every big client, and has an archivist's knowledge of the history of advertising. Probably because they spend so long reading awards annuals.

If that sounds like you, don't worry. There's nothing wrong with you, and you'll be absolutely fine—just make sure you get enough external stimulation, in addition to feeding your advertising addiction, so that your work doesn't become totally self-referential.

At the other end of the scale are the people working in advertising who don't actually like advertising that much. They may even hate it. What they do like is a job where they can write funny sketches, brief composers, and create great images. These people typically have no idea who is the creative director of any given agency, don't know what ads are currently on TV, and couldn't care less whether Cadbury's out-sells Galaxy or goes bankrupt.

That's fine too, and many of our greatest practitioners fall into this category. But if this does sound like you, my one word of caution is that while you don't have to be interested in the ad industry to do well in it, you do have to be interested in the product. If you find your level of interest in advertising is sinking below the water-line, you should probably look to do something else.

The world is a competitive place—to be successful at anything, you have to care.

CHAPTER 9
THE DIFFERING CAREER PATHS OF ART DIRECTORS AND COPYWRITERS

HOW TO BE A GOOD COPYWRITER

In keeping with the rest of the book, this section is not about how to write copy. Instead, it's about the skills and attributes that a good copywriter needs, *above and beyond* being able to write good copy.

In fact, it's debatable whether the ability to write copy is still necessary at all. The demand for copywriting has shrunk massively in the last few years, as print advertising has become increasingly visually driven.

There *are* still examples of great copywriting around, on websites, on packaging, even in-store. But most creatives nowadays come from an art school or graphic design background rather than any kind of writing-related field, and often aren't confident writing copy.

Some creative directors don't mind this, and they keep one or two gray-haired copywriters around specifically to write the department's copy.

But other CDs are hugely frustrated by the shift. And that's why I do think that, if you're not a natural copywriter, it's a good skill to learn. For although the status of copywriting has dropped dramatically within the industry, and there aren't many chances to shine by writing great copy, there is plenty to lose if you write bad copy.

Principally, there's a risk you may displease your creative director. He may be one of the many CDs who places a disproportionate importance on copywriting. This may be because he's an ex-copywriter himself (more copywriters than art directors become CDs; something in the genes?). Or it may be because he's a fair bit older than you—perhaps even of a different generation, in advertising terms, and the older generation seem to place an importance on "proper style," and correct grammar and spelling.

So you may irritate him if you do it badly, and take up his valuable time to help you fix it. If you're never going to be a great writer, at least make sure you can get your copy done quickly and cleanly.

In these days of spell-check and grammar-check, there's no reason to present copy with spelling or grammar mistakes. Even if those things don't matter to you, they may matter to someone else who sees it. Make sure it's right.

TALKING AND LISTENING

As I've mentioned before, the copywriter will often be the "talker" of the team. One stereotype of the copywriter is that he is a smart-ass, always ready with a quip. Certainly, if you want to be original in your work, it helps to be a person who looks at the world skewiff.

Alexandre Gama quotes Kierkegaard, who said: "Any contemporary attempt of getting serious consideration must be expressed through irony."

"Irony is the basic tool of the copywriter's tone-of-voice toolbox," reckons Gama. "The best copywriters are masters of irony. Irony is having fun with the long face of reality."

So if you are a sardonic gagmeister, don't worry. It's common.

Use it to your advantage when you present work. If you are the team's front-man, whether you are the copywriter or not, you need to get good at presenting. Don't be embarrassed to ask for training.

The front-man needs to be good at listening as well as talking. It's much easier to persuade people if you genuinely listen to their point of view, and address it. It will be important to be able to read people too, understand their body language, and "handle" them.

There is normally one person within the team—often but not always the copywriter—who manages the team's career. That means when to ask for a pay rise, when to ask for a promotion, when to move jobs. If it seems like those areas of responsibility are heading your way, learn how to do them well.

INVOLVEMENT IN THE ADVERTISING PROCESS

In terms of the actual job, the copywriter is often more involved at the beginning of the advertising process than the art director is. It seems that copywriters enjoy sparring with planners more than art directors do; in a typical briefing, the copywriter will be asking questions, while the art director doodles on his pad. Either approach is valid, of course—those doodles may turn out to be great ideas. But one of you has to be interrogating the brief, requesting the further information you may need from the account team, and generally being the strategic warhead of the partnership. It doesn't have to be the copywriter; it just often seems to be.

Copywriters are usually more strategically minded than art directors, and there's a high chance that the copywriter will have a greater responsibility for determining what the team's approach to the brief is going to be.

Conversely, the art director is more involved at the *end* of the advertising process. Once an idea has been approved, the art director will spend endless hours choosing photographers and getting layouts ready. What should the copywriter be doing in that time? Starting the next project.

What happens in the middle is less clear-cut. Some creatives believe that a copywriter should be having more ideas—the art director has less time, since the actual production of an ad is so time-consuming. That's certainly true for print. On the other hand, radio tends to fall mostly to the copywriter. And in making a TV commercial, the roles of the art director and copywriter are similar. For some reason, copywriters often seem to be a lot more interested in the editing process than art directors are. And art directors are usually more interested in the "grade" (everything to do with the final look of the ad—like how contrasty or color-saturated the film is). Being a copywriter, it took me three or four years before I even knew what the grade was. And I still fall asleep in there.

IDEAS

I've occasionally heard the theory that art directors have fewer ideas, but the ones they do have are better than the ones that copywriters have.

There is no way to test that theory. What goes on behind closed doors is impossible to know.

Certainly, the number-one complaint that copywriters make about their art directors is *"not enough ideas."*

Copywriters are often rational, logical thinkers, who have a natural facility for coming up with large quantities of ideas, and they can't understand why their art director just sits there like an immovable object, saying nothing except *"no."*

Nevertheless, it's the only combination that seems to work.

I remember years ago, complaining about my art director to a senior creative. *"Just when we seem to be getting somewhere on a brief,"* I said, *"he throws me off track."*

"Ah," came the reply. *"But that's his job."* At the time, I didn't understand. But a few months later I realized what he meant—that without an art director, a copywriter may produce many workable solutions to a brief. But he'll rarely make magic.

HOW TO BE A GOOD ART DIRECTOR

The great art directors can turn an average idea into a good ad, and a good idea into a great ad.

But what skills does an art director need, *above and beyond* being able to art direct?

First of all, just as there are many copywriters nowadays who can't write copy, there are plenty of art directors who can't draw or use a Mac.

This may enrage traditionalists, and cause them to sweep an array of color-coded marker pens off their desk. But it's a reality.

The fact is that since Bill Bernbach first teamed "art men" with copywriters in the 1950s, their role has evolved steadily away from craft skills and more toward concept creation.

THINKING NOT DRAWING

In simple terms, the art director has become a thinker not a drawer. And that's a good thing. Because thinking is more interesting work than drawing, and someone who can think gets paid more than someone who draws.

Of course, *someone* has to draw up the "scamps" for a press campaign—a scamp being a rough drawing whose only purpose is to get the idea across as simply as possible. But some art directors don't even do that. If the team's copywriter happens to be better at drawing than the art director, then it may be the copywriter who draws up.

In my partnership, I often do. Not because I'm any good at drawing, but because he's too good. I'm happy to draw up a rough in 30 seconds even if it looks dreadful, because I know I can't draw and I don't care. Whereas his professional pride means he likes to spend at least five minutes on each drawing, and sometimes we don't have that five minutes.

An art director's main job these days is idea generation —exactly the same as the copywriter's job. Of course, being a visually skilled person, he may approach the task with more visual flair. There's also a theory (completely unverifiable) that the art director comes with a more emotional and instinctive approach, whereas the copy-writer deploys more logic. But I don't believe you can look at a team's output and determine which of their ads were originally the art director's idea and which the copywriter's, because there are plenty of copywriters who are great at visual thinking, especially nowadays, and adept at emotional as well as rationally based selling. Nevertheless, most art directors are people who have a natural facility for creative use of imagery.

ROLES WITHIN THE STUDIO

The art director's role is especially important on a print campaign, where he will choose the photographer or illustrator, and work with a typographer to determine how the type, logo, image, and pack-shot will be put together in the final design of the ad. (There is more information on how to get the best out of photographers and designers in Chapter 6.)

The larger the agency, the more people will be working in their studio—designers, retouchers, per-haps even in-house illustrators. The agency may have further resources such as art buyers, whose job it is to recommend photographers and illustrators to the art director, and picture researchers, who will find you the right stock shot for a print concept. At smaller agencies, and also in certain countries, the art director may carry out some or all of these roles himself.

Many agencies employ a head of art, who acts as a coach and mentor to the junior art directors, and may also have final say over the choice of photographer or illustrator for a project. If your agency has a good head of art, be sure to spend a lot of time with him. The world of visual communication evolves rapidly, but a good head of art will have a lot of wisdom about how to approach that world and get the best out of it, and it's the kind of wisdom you may be able to winkle out if you get to know him well.

THE STEREOTYPE OF AN ART DIRECTOR

In general, art directors are often people who like to *do* more than they like to talk. The cliché of the art director is that he is "arty," colorful, better dressed than the copywriter, a perfectionist when it comes to work, and a party person outside it, much happier on a shoot than sitting in an office talking to a planner about a brief.

By no means all art directors are like that. Just as by no means all copywriters fit the unforgivable string of generalizations I trotted out about them earlier. But it's useful to be aware of the stereotypes, simply so you are aware of whether you're the kind of art director (or copywriter) who fulfills or contradicts people's expectations of the role.

Most art directors are image junkies. They will constantly flick through magazines, be looking at strange things on the internet, go to art galleries in their spare time, and put interesting and beautiful postcards up on their wall.

Fewer art directors seem to go on to become creative directors than copywriters do. Perhaps slightly more go on to become photographers and directors. It's that bias toward doing rather than talking again.

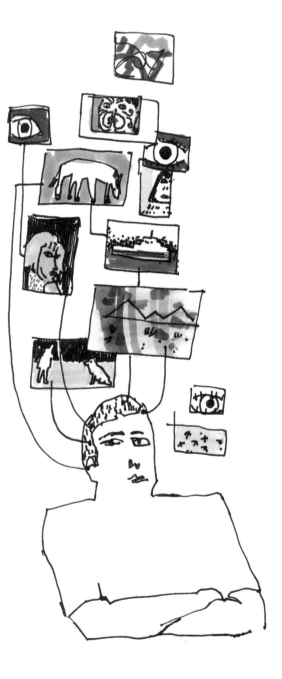

Trevor Beattie

FOUNDER AND CREATIVE DIRECTOR
BEATTIE MCGUINNESS BUNGAY, LONDON, ENGLAND

What do you think are the most important qualities an advertising creative needs above and beyond being able to write good adverts?

Balls of steel. The constitution of an ox. A thick skin. Big ears. An open mind. Bouncebackability. Self-belief. A nice shirt. A childlike sense of wonder at even the most mundane aspects of our world. A sense of humor. A total lack of interest in last year's awards annuals. Oh, and luck. Lots of luck.

The main thing young teams want is simply a job. You are well known for giving young teams their first break—what are the behaviors and attitudes that make you want to hire a team? Why do some people get hired relatively quickly and others take longer, or maybe never get hired at all?

See answer to the first question. But also, so much of it is about timing. Some people are prepared and ready to make it. Some aren't. Some find out that once they've got in, it ain't as easy as they thought/were told it might be. Above all, I never hire people on what's in their book. It's what's in their heads I'm interested in. I can tell from simply talking to a team whether they'll make it or not.

You've worked at big network agencies, successful local agencies, and also start-ups (your own!). Do you think one type of agency is better suited for some people than another, or should anyone be able to work anywhere?

Easy. You should be able to work anywhere and everywhere.

Teamwork. As a CD, can you tell if a team is working well together? Do you think certain sorts of combinations work better than others, or less well? Can an unhappy team do good work?

Yes. An unhappy team can do good work. I disagree with the notion of an "odd couple." All couples should be "odd," i.e. an A and a B. A Lennon and a McCartney. A Yin and Yang. It's when a team start acting alike that their work suffers. They become a pair. They lose perspective.

Is it important for creatives to be good presenters?

It's increasingly important. More and more clients want to meet creative people. If you've created something, you should be proud to show it off, talk it up. Often presenting my work helps me explain the idea more clearly to myself! It can help reveal meanings in the work that you may not have realized existed....

Be afraid.
Be very afraid.

Vote **Labour**
www.labour.org.uk

Is it ever possible to convince a client they are wrong? If so, how?
Only if they are. Do it diplomatically. And only ever face to face.

Which department (TV, traffic, the PAs, planners, or account handlers) is it most important for creatives to have a good relationship with?
It's bloody vital they get on with every single member of the agency. Everyone has a part to play in creating great work.

Do you think any creative can work well in any medium, or are there some teams who will always be a good print team or a good TV team?
Just have great ideas. If they're great enough you'll probably be able to stick 'em anywhere.

Do you approve of creatives doing scam ads/chip shop ads/whatever you want to call them?
No. I call it cheating. It's a hobby, nothing more. An important part of your day job includes convincing a client/company to put their precious money behind your idea in order to flog product. Do your job and stop cheating. There's no future in it and it won't get you a pay rise. And one day you'll get exposed and fired. And I'll laugh. Ha.

Are awards important?

Yes and no. They're rewards rather than awards. Enter them. Win them. But don't build your career around them. And please, please, please, please. Don't display them in your office, you puerile gormless tw*t. (I used to do it, but I'm alright now.) Give 'em to clients. They love 'em. And never, ever, ever, ever, ever, ever take old awards to your new agency. If you see someone doing this, steal the awards and throw them away. Never forget: awards have a date on them. It can become your career's expiry date if you choose to live by them....

When is the right time to move agencies?

Today! (I'm serious. Don't keep putting it off while you finish that shoot you've been waiting to go on....)

It's sometimes said that all the best people have been fired at least once. I understand you were once let go yourself, by BMP, after a merger. Did that have an effect on how you viewed the business, or your career in it?

It was the low point of my entire career. It changed my life for ever. And I vowed it would never ever happen to me again. It hasn't.

You are perhaps the best-known "ad-man" in the UK today. Did you deliberately set out to build a media profile for yourself? Do you think that's an important skill for creatives to learn?

I've never set out to do anything other than my day job. Day-to-day, I tend to make it all up as I go along. It keeps me guessing as much as anyone else. I also have no idea whether that's the right or wrong way to go about things. It just works for me.

You are very active with your outside interests—you have had exhibitions of your memorabilia, and been involved in promoting a rock band and a burlesque show, for example. Would you be worried if a creative had no other interests outside advertising? Another way of phrasing the same question—to be creative do you have to live creative? Is it essential that you love advertising, or is it healthier if your passions lie elsewhere?

Graham Fink has a phrase for it: be a sponge. And he's the most inventive creative director in the business. I suggest we all follow Fink. Advertising itself (and old ads in particular) should be about 0.015 percent of your overall creative influences.

There are a lot of teams nowadays where there is no clear-cut art director/copywriter divide. What's your view on that?

Two heads are better than one. Two silos aren't.

Why do some creatives make it to creative director and others don't?

It's a thankless task. The most difficult and underrated job in our business. Most people want the title, but not the responsibilities (or the endless meetings!) that come with it. Ninety-nine percent of creative directors (especially those at big agencies) are not creative directors. They are group heads. Many of them are technically dick heads. But that's another story. José Mourinho is a brilliant football manager. Yet he never scored a goal in his life. I don't believe you need to have written a decade's worth of brilliant ads to become a great CD. But you do need to be able to recognize and promote great work. Some can. Many can't.

What advice would you have for a creative thinking of starting their own agency?

Stop thinking about it and start doing it.

Finally, when is the right time to get out of advertising?

Getting out of advertising is easy. Just make enough money to walk away and walk away. Getting advertising out of you is a different matter altogether. Most people who've lived their adult lives in advertising (to any degree of success) seem to find it difficult to let go. It's probably best to treat the matter the way you'd treat a start-up: you'll know when the time is right. When it comes, close your eyes and jump. The Geronimo school of career management. Good luck.

MAKING
IT BIG

CHAPTER 10
BECOMING A CREATIVE DIRECTOR

WHY SOME CREATIVES MAKE IT TO CREATIVE DIRECTOR AND OTHERS DON'T

Creative directors have creative responsibility for one or more specific accounts, and are appointed by the agency's ECD (executive creative director), the person in overall charge of the department.

A small agency may not have any CDs at all—the ECD might oversee all the work himself.

But as an agency grows larger, it becomes impossible for the ECD to sign off every piece of work the agency produces, and he is forced to devolve some responsibility.

The main qualification to be a CD is to have done some great work. It's generally felt that people who have come up with good ideas themselves are more likely to be good at spotting them. Also, it's important for a CD's authority that the creatives working under him believe that this person is better than they are. If the creative teams don't have respect for a CD's judgement, it will be hard for him to do his job. So it's normally the best creatives in the department who make creative director.

In other words, CDs are nearly always appointed solely on their creative ability, not their people-management skills. This may sound insane, but it's actually a fairly common state of affairs in every sphere of life. The best scientist in a lab will tend to get made the next lab manager, whatever his managerial abilities.

And once they become a CD, they discover it's completely different to the job of being a creative, and requires a different skill-set. Most adapt fine. But just as it's not necessarily the best footballers who make the best managers, it's not necessarily the best creatives who make the best CDs.

QUALITIES THAT MAKE A GOOD CREATIVE DIRECTOR

The job of CD is fantastic fun, but it's also difficult and time-consuming—you need to be a planner, account man, and creative all rolled into one.

You are also leaving your carefree days behind. A regular creative is free to present the most outrageous idea he can think of; the creative director needs to be able to see the bigger picture, like the client's overall business problem.

You are responsible for creative quality on the account that you look after: that means you mustn't present work that is dull. But on the other hand, if you exclusively present work that the client can't or won't approve, you will come to a sticky end.

This tricky balancing act leads some CDs to conclude they are best off writing the ads themselves, rather than relying on their teams. And sometimes you'll have to. But I strongly advise you not to write ads in competition with the teams who are working into you as a CD. Nothing enrages and demotivates creatives more. Quite simply, creatives don't believe you will ever pick their ad in preference to yours. So if they get wind that you are working on the brief in competition with them, they'll stop trying. Your job is to get them to do their job, not to do it yourself.

CHAMPIONING OTHERS' WORK

To be a successful CD, you have to enjoy seeing other people write great ads, and enjoy helping them improve their ideas. (Or if they don't have an idea, subtly suggesting one to them. You've got to be willing to give. Even if it's a great idea from your own bottom drawer.)

So that's the first thing to realize about becoming a CD—you must be happy to champion someone else's work. Creatives are a selfish bunch, on the whole. Our main reason for wanting to do good work is for our own fame and glory. And salary.

But a CD must have a different way of thinking. He has to shield, protect, and nurture work that he hasn't created himself. He has to fight for it, defend it, and try and make it the best it can be. All for someone else's fame and glory.

If you're slightly insecure, as most creatives are, this can be hard.

One acquaintance of mine confessed he thought he was a rubbish CD because it annoyed him when someone showed him something good that he hadn't done himself!

Another well-known CD would positively fume if anyone produced work that was praised more highly than his own or, God forbid, won awards when his didn't. He even used to think it funny if a team got Turkey of the Week in *Campaign*. He once moaned that he hadn't got any ads in D&AD one year. When it was pointed out to him that at least a dozen pieces of work were in, with him as CD, he simply said "doesn't count." His job was CD but he never stopped behaving like an AD.

The best CDs love it when someone brings them a great idea. And so they should—it makes their job easy.

SPOTTING A GOOD IDEA

Being able to spot a good idea is, at the risk of stating the obvious, the first requirement of the job.

It's much easier in certain media, like posters, where the "rough" that the creative team presents is nearer to the finished ad than a TV script is to a finished commercial. But even in the case of posters, it's rare for a creative team to walk in with an obviously brilliant idea, leaving the CD with a task no more arduous than giving the thumbs-up sign.

Most ideas are first presented in an undeveloped, half-baked, or embryonic state. Spotting the embryos that could grow into beautiful children isn't easy.

Some ideas might have a logical core to them, but are prosaic in the form they're expressed in. That's when you can make someone's ad leap from 4/10 to 9/10 with a wave of your wand.

And sometimes an idea that seems weird, crass, or simplistic can make an amazing ad. If someone presented you with a script that read: "A gorilla in a recording studio listens to 'In the Air Tonight' by Phil Collins, and joins in on the drum solo"…would you buy it?

"Trust your gut instinct and stick to it," advises James Cooper, creative director at Dare New York. "It's really the only weapon you have. You have split seconds to make a decision on a piece of work and sometimes people. If you don't have much of a gut instinct you're probably a little screwed."

TOP TEN TRAITS OF A GREAT CD

1. Still has something to prove, rather than banging on about ads he made ten years ago.
2. Guides with tact, without undermining teams' confidence.
3. Is sometimes scary.
4. Kills a team's work but sends them away inspired to do more.
5. Is a political genius.
6. Is 20 percent party starter, 10 percent defender of his teams, 5 percent politician, 5 percent dictator, 10 percent media sponge, 50 percent ideas fountain.
7. A great judge of work, and a great presenter of work.
8. Doesn't just say "No," but also "Why."
9. Brings out the best in his teams, but without doing their work for them.
10. Knows when to tell a team "the suits are right on this one," but also knows when to tell the suits to toe the line.

You need to be comfortable with people doing things you wouldn't do. A lot of creatives have a strong style, and want to impose it on all the work that they creative-direct. That's a mistake. You don't want to force people to be clones of you. They'll never do "you" as well as you do. And they won't enjoy being made to.

Just look for a simple thought, clearly expressed, with a degree of irreverence or freshness that will stand out in whatever medium it appears.

In addition, try to work out how well an idea answers the brief. That's not to say that every idea you sign off has to be completely on-brief. But be aware how much "persuasion" you may need to do, and how much leeway you have on that particular brief or with that particular client.

OTHER MAN-MANAGEMENT SKILLS

Good CDs have a talent for persuasion. After spotting the potential in an idea, you need the skill to persuade other people of its potential too. It's not enough to just tell account teams *This ad is great,"* or to fall back on your authority and explain that this is the one you've gone for, and that's the end of the conversation. You need to be able to bring people along with you.

Great relationships make great advertising.

And to make a great relationship, you need to learn the rules of compromise. Don't try to win every battle. One of the hardest things about being a CD is learning to compromise. Some of the best creative people are uncompromising. But now you can't be. Now, you have to ask yourself *"What do they want, and how do I make it good?"*

Be a person of principle and integrity. Lying to get your way might be effective in that particular situation, but once people find out you've lied, you'll lose their trust.

Creatives need to trust that you will do your best to support their idea and only surrender when further fight is pointless. The account team needs to trust that you are a team player and will help them overcome client concerns. And the client needs to trust that you are creating work for their consumers, not an awards jury.

"Get clients to trust you have their best interests at heart, not a lump of yellow wood," is how Justin Tindall, ECD of The Red Brick Road, puts the point.

These are just some of the considerable man-management skills you will need. Tact, consideration for others, and an ability to listen are a few others that spring to mind.

You'll also need to be a good talker, since a CD's job consists mostly of talking. Rank-and-file creatives can get away with being virtually silent if they do good work, but CDs need to be good at communicating their thinking face to face, not just via the medium of posters or TV ads or whatever. You need to be able to give creative teams feedback and support, and present to clients and account teams.

Finally, a good CD is someone with the ability to inspire. It could be through the work they've produced, or simply how they make teams feel who are working into them. This is the most important man-management skill of all—knowing how to get the best out of teams. Some need talking-up to perform to their best. Others need a good old kick up the backside.

"Your main job is adding momentum to projects," Rob Reilly, ECD at Crispin Porter + Bogusky USA, told *Creativity* magazine. "Creatives that are stuck, you have to keep their momentum going. And when you're pitching something, the same. We're the momentum makers."

"There are basically two kinds of creative directors," believes Jamie Barrett, ECD at Goodby Silverstein, San Francisco. "The kind that tries to bully and intimidate and pressure people into doing good work. And the kind that tries to nurture and support and inspire. When you first become a creative director, you just need to decide which kind you want to be."

BECOMING EXECUTIVE CREATIVE DIRECTOR

As we've seen, creative directors are appointed by the executive creative director. But who appoints the ECD?

One of the fascinating things about becoming ECD is that, after spending your entire career learning how to impress creative chiefs, you now need to get hired by a completely different set of characters: agency CEOs, chairmen, and heads of planning. Interestingly, this makes the ECD the only creative in the building not hired by another creative.

There are a few exceptions—some agency networks employ a worldwide creative director whose job includes hiring ECDs for agencies within the group. But in most cases, it's the agency management themselves who bring in the ECD.

This means that getting an ECD position is about a lot more than just your creative credentials. To get the job you will need to be able to sit with the agency's bosses and talk coherently about the *business* of advertising. You will need a point of view on where it's been, where it's at, and where it's going.

You will need to have a high profile in the industry, so they can present you to the outside world as someone with creative credibility. Someone who will attract good talent.

You may think there's a danger that agency bosses will want to employ someone malleable. Indeed, some observers suggest there has been a trend toward the "pragmatic" ECD, even the politician. One London ECD certainly thinks this is the case. *"The old ECDs weren't good managers, but they did a better job with the work,"* he believes.

But one agency head of planning, who is currently going through the process of hiring an ECD, denies this completely.

"We want a grown-up," he told me, "but not someone pliant. We're looking for a leader…someone with charisma. The ECD should be the biggest character in the room."

"Who is the person who will make our agency more successful in the future? That's our number-one criterion," he adds.

An ECD must be someone who can get the best out of their department, whether that's by creating a culture where creativity can flourish, or simply by setting the bar high.

"I don't try to change the culture," Gerry Graf, chief creativity officer of Saatchi & Saatchi NY, told *Creativity* magazine. "I don't know how to inspire people. I've given countless speeches and feel like an idiot every time I talk into a mic. My job is to make really good creative and I try to do that. And let that inspire people."

"To evolve people, you have to stretch them," says Dave Dye, creative partner of Dye Holloway Murray. *"You have to give people things to do that they've never done before, things that are just in front of them. And that's scary."*

And you have to enjoy looking after a group of people, and get a kick out of them doing well.

"The night every team at DDB (bar one!) won a silver at Campaign Press was better than any night when I won myself," remarks Ewan Paterson, former joint ECD of DDB London, now ECD of Clemmow Hornby Inge.

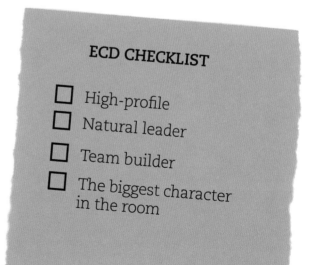

ECD CHECKLIST

☐ High-profile
☐ Natural leader
☐ Team builder
☐ The biggest character in the room

The final point is that of all the employees in the agency, the ECD has the most latitude to do his job how he wants. You can be a nit-picking micro-manager or a laid-back embodiment of bonhomie; you can puke in a carrier bag in front of the people who call you boss, or live like a monk; you can CD via in-tray and out-tray or spend half an hour explaining why a comma beats a semi-colon; you can be an industry figure or a shrinking violet; you can love the suits or show them healthy disdain; you can go home at 5am or 5pm; you can let your department work in the pub or insist everyone clocks in and out; you can have a penis or a vagina or both. All of the above have worked; all that matters is how good the ads are.

And that will mostly depend on who you hire to do them.

"If you have terrific people, the advertising business isn't that difficult," says Bob Hoffman, founder of US agency Hoffman/Lewis. "If you have mediocrities, advertising is impossible. For your own self-preservation you must get rid of bad people and hire good ones. There is no other way to do good work and have a happy life."

HIRING

"Recruit people who've created a campaign (not a one-off) from a blank sheet of paper," is the tip from Ewan Paterson. "Don't recruit the person who's done the next award-winning ad in an award-winning campaign (that someone else created). And if you can find people who've done that in an agency that doesn't normally produce great work, then all the better. And on top of that they have to be nice people."

"Hire keen unknowns who want to make a name for themselves," suggests another ECD. *"Bring in students, or people working in unfashionable agencies."*

Whatever your philosophy, you have to be good at spotting talent.

Tony Cox, the former BMP executive creative director, used to say that recruiting for a creative department should be like casting for the perfect cocktail party. Once you have the right people, all the ECD need do is wander around making sure everyone's drinks are topped up.

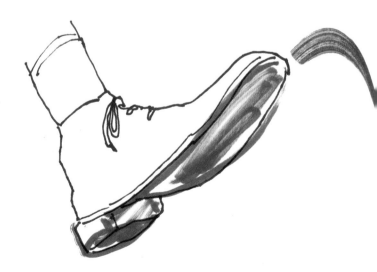

FIRING

The flipside of hiring, of course, is firing.

> "The day I arrived at Y&R New York it was announced that we had lost both Sony and Jaguar, over $300 million worth of business," Matt Eastwood, national creative director of DDB Australia, told _ihaveanidea.org_. "After only weeks in the job, I was asked to draw up a list of creative people that would be let go. It was one of the most depressing and disappointing moments in my career."

Every ECD agrees that this is one of the hardest aspects of the job. "_But every time you do it, you get better at it,_" consoles Dave Dye.

> "_Always try and treat people how you'd want to be treated yourself," says Ewan Paterson. "I try to approach the horrible bits of the job by saying to myself—I'm going to do this in the best way possible._"

Paul Arden got fired five times before he found his niche at Saatchi's, and stayed there for 17 years. So maybe there's no need to feel too bad about firing someone. If it's not working out for them at your agency, maybe they'll do well somewhere else. And if they end up proving you wrong, good for them.

NEGOTIATING YOUR PACKAGE AND SHARE OPTIONS

There's one simple piece of advice that every ECD will give you about negotiating your package—get a lawyer.

You're an expert in your field; clients rely on you for your expertise. In the same way, you have to be able to acknowledge areas you're _not_ an expert in.

Negotiating a package that may include bonus triggers, share options, golden handcuffs (and a potential golden parachute—i.e. a pay-off if they decide they want to dispense with your services) is a complex transaction. Don't try to do it on your own. If you don't know who to use, lean on the relationships you've made in your time in advertising—ask around.

Naturally you're delighted to get a big job, and a big opportunity. But go into it with your eyes open. Be thorough about your contract. Get your lawyer to explain everything to you fully.

Creatives are notoriously bad at the business side of things, and have been somewhat exploited by people who know about money. Don't let that be the case with you. Have a sense of your own value, and negotiate hard. You'll be surprised what you can get, if you ask.

Amir Kassaei

CHIEF CREATIVE OFFICER
DDB GERMANY

You were born in Iran, grew up in Austria, took higher education in France...and now work in Germany. Do you think exposure to multiple cultures gives a creative person an advantage, or is it possible to be highly creative without ever leaving one's home town?

It's not really about where you live: But a global point of view—not only geographically, but in the sense of a very broad horizon—is more than helpful. The wider your perspective, the more it is probable you will produce innovations.

You were a CD at 33, and became chief creative officer of the entire DDB Group in Germany at only 37. Was your youth ever a problem?

No. It's not the theoretical age that matters. It's about your level of maturity and also about your social and emotional competence.

What makes a good creative team?

A good team generates more than the sum of each individual's talents. And each individual complements the other in terms of talent, character, and skills.

Is it important for creatives to be good presenters?

Yes. Only creatives know how an idea has been developed and why this idea is the best solution for a specific problem. Creatives are the only ones who have the passion and energy that is needed for selling an idea.

Scam ads—a great way for creatives to learn, and showcase their talents; or a form of cheating that needs to be stamped out?

It is part of our job to have fun and try something new. Nevertheless, the main mission is to solve our clients' problems. Having both components in balance is fine. But if you start becoming overly proud of finding solutions to non-existent problems, you will have missed your target in respect of your primary mission.

You are said to have won over 500 awards. Are awards important?

In the strict sense there have been more than 1,400 awards! But: no. Awards are a welcome confirmation that you are right. But nothing more.

In interviews you talk a lot about change and the future. You've said that "our competition now is Google" and you've talked about "getting away from ancient ways of working." It sounds like you are finding that many creatives—even at a young age—are rather fixed in their attitudes and ways of working...?

Yes, because 99 percent of all creatives in the world are still producing advertising ideas instead of creative solutions. Advertising ideas help less and less in solving the client's real marketing problems.

You have a high media profile. Did you make a deliberate decision to build one? Do you think it's an important skill for creatives to learn?

If you are claiming you are qualified in strategic brand management, you should understand the importance of nourishing and cultivating your own brand. But don't make yourself more important than your last piece of work.

A final word?

If we creatives don't manage to develop and change from communication service providers to creative consultants within the next five years, we will not have the right to exist.

POLITICS

Politics, in a business context, has become a dirty word. And to describe someone as "political" is a major insult. This is foolish. We all know that there's far more to doing your job well than just keeping your head down and doing a good job.

> Machiavelli defined politics as *"the art of getting and keeping power and authority."*
> It's essential that you master this art. Not in an underhand or Machiavellian way, necessarily. But you need to know how to maintain your power and authority.

First of all, you can't do your job at all if you get sacked, so you need to keep on the right side of whoever can sack you.

"*Many excellent creative people have been ejected from agencies as a convenient scapegoat for account losses,*" former AMV and Ogilvy CD Paul Belford points out. "*Or simply because a new chief executive wanted to stamp their authority on the place.*"

And secondly, you need to have a certain amount of power and autonomy to do the job the way you want to do it, else you will suffer inordinate frustration.

MANAGING UPWARD AS WELL AS DOWNWARD

The best piece of advice that ECDs I have spoken to on the question of politics give is to make sure that you manage upward as well as downward.

Managing downward is what your contract says you should do. That is, getting great work out of your department. But managing upward is equally important to your long-term future at the agency. And it can put you in a difficult position. For example, imagine a conversation with a senior agency management person where they explicitly ask for, let's say, not exactly cutting-edge work on certain accounts. It happens. Not because they really want rubbish work but because they're terrified of losing the income from a difficult client. You can see their point.

So, in that instance, the creative director's job is not to ensure that the work is as good as the talent in the creative department can produce. It is to produce the best work that the client is capable of buying. And of course, sub-standard work can always be held against you in the future. So what do you do? It's a dilemma.

Treading the fine line between doing the right thing creatively and not coming into conflict with your chief executive, managing director, planning director, and any number of other senior account people can be extremely difficult. You'll only pull it off by having good relationships with these people and the clients. And that's what managing upward is.

CHAPTER 11
STARTING YOUR OWN AGENCY

THE RIGHT TIME AND THE WRONG TIME TO DO IT

"There are pros and cons to starting [an agency] at different times in your career," argues Owen Lee, creative partner at Farm Communications in London. "When you're younger, you have more energy, less cynicism, and probably more time, if you don't have children for instance. However, if you are established in the industry, you have far more contacts and clients you can approach. If I had to call it, I'd say about ten years' experience in the industry is ideal, but people have made a success of it both earlier and later. I think fate plays a hand in when you set up, certain things come together—the right people, the right client, the right redundancy package."

"Fame and success can be a rewarding consequence, but they are not the best motivation for starting an agency," warns Alexandre Gama, president and chief creative officer of Neogama BBH (Brazil). *"In my case, independence was the motivation...but in the end you become dependent on clients' decisions and approvals anyway."*

"There isn't a right time, just less wrong times," suggests Jo Tanner, co-founder of creative boutique Us London. "But don't ever expect all the boxes will be ticked because if they appear to be...that's a sure sign you're in for a surprise. It will always feel like jumping into cold water to some degree—and that doesn't half make you feel alive."

José Molla, co-founder of La Comunidad, Miami, told *ihaveanidea.org*: "I always obeyed my intuition. I never let rationality prevail, no matter how attractive the offer was. At one point I simply felt that it was time to make the leap. I had shot commercials all over the world with top directors, I had worked in three offices, I was single, and was well off financially. It was just the time to do it. I went to talk to Dan Wieden and told him, "after working here I cannot go back to work in a traditional agency. I am going to have to open my own agency." Everyone would tell me I was insane; why would I leave a job like that? We opened without having any clients. I will never forget when I spoke with my lawyer regarding some paperwork and I told her I had to discuss it with the office staff and that I would get back to her. I hung up the phone and found myself alone in the office, with no one to discuss anything. That's when change hit me. Now things depended on me."

WHO DO YOU START AN AGENCY WITH - PEOPLE YOU LIKE OR PEOPLE YOU THINK ARE GREAT?

"Preferably both," says Owen Lee, "but definitely people you think are great. You do spend a lot of time and go through a lot of highs and lows with your business partners, so it's good if you like them, but pivotal that you think they are good at what they do. Perhaps rather than people you like, people you trust is more important."

Justin Tindall, creative partner at The Red Brick Road in the UK, agrees on the importance of trust.

"You have to have confidence in every member of the team," is Justin Tindall's view. "If you lose a few pitches in a row, your relationship is going to get tested, so there needs to be a mutual respect. But most of all, there needs to be a shared point of view. You need people with the same values."

"They need to be people you like and who are great," says Ben Priest, the founding creative partner of Adam & Eve, which launched in London in 2008.

"But if I had to choose, 'great' would win every time. I have plenty of friends who work outside of the business; I don't need more mates, just people who are brilliant at what they do. It really helps if some or all of you have worked together before. For us that was a huge reassurance; our relationships had already survived long, long hours and pressure. Think of it as going to war—who would you want at the front with you? However, I would say one or a few of you need enough of a profile to get new business momentum."

"Do it with people you trust," echoes Jo Tanner. "And make no mistake, that trust will be tested way beyond Recommended Industry Standard Tolerances."

"The only thing that matters in a start-up is that everyone involved gets on and respects each other," says Ben Kay, who was the initial co-creative director of Lunar BBDO, UK, but left in 2008.

"Otherwise the tiny cracks of difference at the beginning will eventually resemble the Grand Canyon, and by then you'll be in too deep to separate painlessly. This also is very important because potential clients smell disagreement a mile off and will not give you their business."

Mark Denton, former creative partner of legendary 1990s UK hotshop Simons Palmer Denton Clemmow & Johnson, recalls;

"We got a phone call from Paul Simons, we met him, and then we met Simon Clemmow and Carl Johnson, and they liked our reel. So then we went into business with these guys...but we didn't even know who they were. It was completely naïve. And in fact we never took the time to get to know them. So it was no surprise when we fell out six-and-a-half years later. It was a very costly slap around the legs."

"Don't be tempted to do a start-up where your other partners are all creatives," advises Dave Dye, whose first UK agency, Campbell Doyle Dye, fitted that description, and eventually folded in 2008. "It doesn't work. Who makes the calls? One CD is much better."

TOP TEN TIPS FOR STARTING YOUR OWN AGENCY

1 Picking a good time helps. As does having a client already. But having great partners is the key.
2 Make sure you trust these people totally. You're putting your house on the line for them.
3 Don't do it when you're young and inexperienced. But don't leave it till you're old and bitter either.
4 As with starting a rock band, the name you choose is crucial. A creative name like "Mother" or "Santo" communicates "We're creative"; a shop named after the founding partners says "We're professionals."
5 Choose your location and décor with care; they will start to define you.
6 Don't be completely ignorant of the business side of doing a start-up. But don't try to handle it yourself.
7 Be prepared to become so busy that your family forgets what you look like.
8 Only go after the clients you want. If they don't offer either good money or good creative opportunity, say thanks but no thanks.
9 Be honest about whether you really are an entrepreneurial person. There's no shame in opting for the comfort of air miles and international board meetings instead.
10 You could build an incredible business, but you could also lose all your savings. How does that feel? If you answered "exhilarating," you're ready to jump.

WHY DO SOME START-UPS SUCCEED AND OTHERS DISAPPEAR?

Francesco Taddeucci, formerly creative director at Saatchi & Saatchi Roma, now creative director and co-founder of The Name, has a piece of advice for that all-important question—what to call your agency.

"If you're not sure what to name your agency," he says, "remember this: all agency names are bad… until you do a great piece of work. In general, starting your own agency is stupendously exciting, but the effort is double—your mind is involved 100 percent of the time. Be prepared for that. But don't panic: clients will follow quality. And if that even happens in Italy, it happens everywhere else in the world, believe me."

"If you can't be brutally honest with yourself and each other, and be humble enough to learn from the inevitable mistakes that happen along the way, then your business will fail," says Ben Priest. *"Lots of important people in advertising already think they know everything. That's a disaster when you're starting your own business."*

"Many a great player in a big agency has discovered how hard it is to suddenly be exposed to hunting around for clients yourself, writing the ads, selling the ads, and talking about the state of the agency toilets," says Owen Lee. "I remember having a conversation with Richard Flintham just after they had started Fallon London about how much layout pads cost—I'm sure the average stellar creative in a big agency doesn't even know where you'd buy a layout pad, let alone how much they go for. Running your own agency simply isn't for everyone. It certainly isn't the Promised Land that many people in big agencies think it might be."

"A key founding client is perhaps the most important ingredient for success," Lee continues. "A client where the relationship is so strong that they feel they have a vested interest in your success. And of course it gives you an income stream. Think of CHI and Carphone Warehouse, VCCP and O2, Red Brick Road and Tesco, BMB and French Connection."

Campbell Doyle Dye launched with a large founding client—Mercedes—and Dave Dye's new agency, Dye Holloway Murray, launched without a founding client, so he has experienced both scenarios.

"If you have backing, the new agency can feel like a "little big agency" rather than a genuine start-up," he believes. "With no backing, no money coming in, your house on the line, it feels totally different. You're wired. But it forces you to have a philosophy."

"You must set out a set of values for your business," agrees Alexandre Gama. *"This is a controversial and difficult matter, but if you don't stand for something, you'll fall for anything."*

Ben Kay, on the other hand, doesn't believe a philosophy is required. "You will spend an inordinate amount of time trying to work out what kind of agency you want to be," he says. "Don't bother. Accept that you all want to do good work (if that's what you want to do; making money can be equally/ more motivating) and do your jobs to that end."

Paul Silburn

EXECUTIVE CREATIVE DIRECTOR
SAATCHI & SAATCHI, LONDON, ENGLAND

What do you think are the most important qualities an advertising creative needs—above and beyond being able to write good adverts?

If you've got the ability you just need tons and tons of luck.

What did you learn at college that helps you today?

I didn't go to college or university. I left school because I hated it and didn't know what I wanted to do with myself for some time. I hated being told what to do, and if I'm honest I still do. I had a few pointless day jobs while trying to get into record companies and doing some DJing. The only things I was half good at while at school were messing about and writing, so eventually I decided to try and use them in some way but didn't consider advertising at first. I learned how to put a book together by seeing creatives in agencies. It took ages because I was so naïve. I suppose what I learnt from this is that I should have gone to college.

You're British but you've spent time as a CD in the US. Do you think anyone should be able to work anywhere, or do you think certain people are more suited to certain countries or cities?

In theory, anyone should now be able to work anywhere, but it really depends on the circumstances, culture, and politics of each agency at the time. That's true whether you're simply changing from getting off the tube at a different stop in London or moving thousands of miles to a different country.

After several successful years working with the renowned art director Tiger Savage, the two of you went through a painful and public "divorce." Do you have any advice about creative partnerships?

Ummm...not really.

You're known for successful collaborations with directors; for example you've worked with Danny Kleinman on both the John West "Bear" and the John Smith's Peter Kay campaign. Any tips for getting the best out of directors?

Write them a great script.

Do you think any creative can work well in any medium, or are there some teams who will always be "a good print team" or "a good TV team"?

There's no doubt some creatives excel in certain areas. I don't know why that is, but does it matter? If it does it's a bit like expecting a brilliant striker to also be a great goalkeeper.

Scam ads—a great way for creatives to learn, and showcase their talents; or a form of cheating that needs to be stamped out?

I'm not impressed by scam. I used to admire the fact that some creatives would go out and do stuff on their own initiative, but it's become a complete joke now. What staggers me is that some very senior people have made a fortune and got some very highly paid and important positions on the back of this kind of work; that makes me disillusioned at times.

Are awards important?

They're obviously crucial to the senior people I referred to above. My view is that it's nice to be recognized for doing something that people love—but it means most to me if it's working and loved by the public too. I like winning awards, but forget it the day after the ceremony and get on with the next project. I'm not into putting the gross-looking things on shelves to show off how many I have. In fact, I shipped all my awards in boxes to the US and back to the UK without ever unpacking them and realized I never would. So I took the lot (minus the D&AD pencils my wife made me keep and a Cannes Lion, which we use as a doorstop in our living room) and dumped them at the local council tip.

I understand you have a passion for music…is it essential for a creative to love advertising, or is it healthier if their passions lie elsewhere?

I think you really have to love what you do to get the best out of yourself and from the industry. But that doesn't mean you can't have outside interests like music, art galleries, movies, TV, books…and surfing YouTube.

GETTING THE RIGHT FINANCING AND LEGAL ADVICE

"The finance and legal stuff is tedious and tiresome," says Jo Tanner. *"Don't let enthusiasm carry you away. Don't say you'll do the VAT returns unless you absolutely mean it. Better to pay someone who actually likes doing that stuff."*

"Know that being a creative has nothing to do with running an agency," says Alexandre Gama. *"Very different skills. So, unless you have both abilities (rare), never try a creative approach with the finance department, for instance. Have a very, very conservative policy there."*

"This is a steep learning curve," says Owen Lee. "It's invaluable to have a business person on your team that you trust (usually the finance director). It's not just creatives; I think account people and planners also come to the crushing realization that we know how to create advertising but we haven't got a clue how the business runs. But you learn. Usually by mistakes. The learning curve gets even steeper when you eventually sell the company."

The importance of sound legal and business advice is underlined by Mark Denton. *"I got kicked out of my own agency, despite having won a ton of awards,"* he recounts.

"Creatives must protect themselves," says Ben Kay. *"Make sure you can't be voted out by your partners. Set up a system whereby unanimous decisions are needed for such important occurrences."*

WHAT TYPES OF BUSINESS TO PITCH FOR AND THE ONES TO AVOID

"At first you think the phone will never ring," says Ben Priest. "You fear your wife and kids will starve, and you want to go for everything. But very, very quickly you realize—for your soul and sanity—you have to be selective. It's really a people thing—do you like the clients, can you imagine spending time with them trying to hammer out something brilliant?"

"At the beginning, you are so hungry to prove yourself that you end up chasing every ball like a six-year-old playing football," admits Owen Lee. *"We've all chased ridiculous pitches."*

"You learn. You will develop antennae for time-wasters and something-for-nothingers," says Jo Tanner. *"There are a lot out there."*

"We did letterheads at the beginning," confesses Dave Dye. "We did anything. But we always tried to make it good – we never did big logos and dumbed-down work. A lot of start-ups focus on winning tons of business first, and then make the work better later. In a way, I don't criticize that attitude. You can't improve the creative work if you don't exist."

"When it's your own business, you naturally become more responsible," he explains. "You don't tell a client 'I absolutely have to have a one-legged man in this commercial, or it doesn't work.' You're a bit more sensible. You become thoughtful about what the client really needs, not just what you want to do for them."

"Nothing goes the way you think it will," warns Dave Dye, finally.

"It's like jumping in a fast-flowing river—you just have to move and react. But I could never go back to a big agency now."

CHAPTER 12
GETTING OUT

There aren't many old creatives.

Before they get old, most creatives seem to leave. But the question of where they go and what they do has never been satisfactorily answered.

However, the three most common exits seem to be Up & Out, Down & Out, and Deciding To Do Something Else.

UP AND OUT

Successful creatives who go on to become creative directors or start their own agencies eventually get "squeezed out of the top" of the business.

Creatives who start their own agency normally do so for the thrill and the autonomy. But after about five years of bloody hard work, they will (assuming things have gone well) get offers to sell. They may say no—the challenge of growing the agency to the next level may be compelling. But if their agency continues to do well, eventually the amount of money offered becomes too good to turn down.

After the sale (normally to a big agency network that is looking for an infusion of creativity) there is often an "earn-out period," during which the founders must remain in place to steer the agency through the next few years, and in return will receive an additional tranche of money if certain business targets are met.

After the earn-out, the founding creative director normally doesn't want to work full-time any more, and will usually step back from the day-to-day running of the company, though he may take up a consultative role, while pursuing his interests in art, fine wine, or similar. (There are some notable exceptions—Sir John Hegarty, who co-founded BBH, is still the first creative to arrive in the department every morning, every day of the week.)

Big agency ECDs often seem to end up in a global role that involves being more of a figurehead than a working creative director, and eventually get fired in return for a large pay-off, or—just possibly—they retire. Whichever is the case, by now he is normally happy with what he has done, and doesn't need to do it any more, either financially or emotionally.

But for many creatives, unfortunately, the time of leaving is not so peaceful.

DOWN AND OUT

Creative departments are designed in a pyramid structure. There is one ECD at the top, several creative directors underneath him and several teams under each of them.

Simple math dictates that, every year, some creatives get fired.

No figures are available, but I'd estimate that only one in ten creatives makes it to creative director, and one in 50 to ECD.

If you don't make it up to the next level of the pyramid, it is possible to stay for quite a while on the level that you are on. But each year, a new generation of students graduate from advertising college, a new generation of juniors are becoming middleweights, and a new generation of middleweights are becoming senior creatives.

So eventually, you will be overtaken by someone younger and cheaper. Apologies if that sounds a bit bleak. But it's no different to the structure of any other profession, such as journalism, accountancy, investment banking, or the law. A newspaper, for example, has only one editor, a few section heads, and many reporters.

As I've mentioned before, many creatives who get fired can simply get a job in a slightly less good agency. And this can go on for a while. But eventually, they can't get another job, and they are forced to do something else.

Or, creatives make an active choice to do something else, either because they've got pissed off with advertising, or they've realized there's something else they want to do more.

DECIDING TO DO SOMETHING ELSE

Jobs that creatives do after advertising include writing books, lecturing on advertising, e-commerce projects, raising pigs, running artsy magazines, acupuncture, and poetry-writing. We're a varied bunch, so it's to be expected that our alternative career paths are varied too.

There are many ex-creatives who have found fame as novelists. These include Joseph Heller (author of *Catch-22*), Salman Rushdie (ex-Ogilvy London, wrote the Booker Prize-winning *Midnight's Children*), Peter Carey (Australian ex-copywriter, twice winner of the Booker Prize), and Don DeLillo (author of *Falling Man*), who worked for five years at Ogilvy NY.

In the world of film, our alumni include Alan Parker (ex-copywriter at CDP, subsequently directed movies including *Bugsy Malone* and *Mississippi Burning*), Tony Kaye (another ex-CDP creative, since has directed *American History X*), Andrew Niccol (formerly creative director at BBDO London, went on to write the screenplay for *The Truman Show*, and wrote and directed *Gattaca*), and John Hughes (was a copywriter in Chicago, before directing *The Breakfast Club* and *Ferris Bueller's Day Off*).

But probably the most common "next career" for creatives is commercials directing. Mark Denton, co-founder of celebrated London hotshop Simons Palmer Denton Clemmow & Johnson, is now a successful ad director.

He transitioned gradually into the role. *"When there wasn't a proper budget for a job, Chris [Palmer] and I ended up directing things ourselves."*

Does he miss being a creative?

"Sometimes. I miss the cut-and-thrust and the camaraderie. Except…I do notice that things have changed. Like showing the client three recommendations for an ad. And all the planning. I don't know if I'd survive now."

"It's a short career," he adds. "Unless you learn how to play the game."

Some creatives go on to set up a non-advertising-related business. This is especially true in Asia, with its highly entrepreneurial culture, where it's quite common to have a second string to your bow. There are creative directors with restaurants, art directors with a designer bag sideline, and copywriters who are also part-time journalists. An ECD from Leo Burnett in Bangkok went on to set up a successful chain of clothing stores.

David Hieatt was a highly regarded copywriter at Abbott Mead Vickers BBDO in London, before setting up the organic clothing company Howies.

He believes there is rarely a "right time" to leave advertising if you have some other dream or passion you want to follow.

"The stars don't just suddenly all line up in a row," says David. "The leap of faith has to be taken without any guarantees. In the taking-off of a plane, there is a point on the runway called V1. This is the point of no return. Once the plane has passed this point on the runway, it has to take off. It is a physical line. But we are not so lucky to have a line like that. Ours is an imaginary line that just exists in our heads. The point where not following our dream becomes more painful than following someone else's."

David doesn't miss advertising. But he does miss "playing football on Friday with my mates."

Mississippi Burning (1988), directed by former copywriter Alan Parker.

While you're earning a good living and having fun, advertising is a wonderful industry to be in, and I'd recommend staying as long as you can.

But when you lose your mojo or it's no longer fun or there's something else you want to do more…there's a whole world out there.

No one stays in advertising for ever.

But almost no one regrets having done it.

Bob Isherwood quit his role as worldwide creative director of Saatchi & Saatchi in 2008, citing a need to have "more than one life in my lifetime. For the past 12 years I've been focused on the reinvention of Saatchi & Saatchi," he told *Ad Age* from his home in Miami. "Now I've reached a point where I feel a need to reinvent myself."

Paul Burke is another former copywriter who has since become a successful writer. "Having dealt with publishers, I now love ad agencies," says Paul. "Publishers are useless and nice, whereas ad agencies are efficient and nice."

"I miss the companionship," adds Paul. "You can stroll into people's offices, whereas you can't do that when you're working at home. But I don't miss agency life. I find it more creative and productive to be out and about."

Bill Green, the US art director and founder of popular ad blog _Make the Logo Bigger_, believes few creatives actually leave the industry. "Most form their own shops and move out of the major metropolitan areas, starting over with something smaller. (I suspect they do this after the politics of a large agency get to them.) Two former writers from Leo Burnett struck a deal to create _Trust Me_, a US cable TV show about the biz, but that's rare."

Tim Harris, an English former copywriter turned author, believes that the right time to leave is "simply if or when you feel more enthusiastic about doing something else that can't be combined with advertising."

"I don't miss advertising," adds Tim, "but that's probably because I use the skills every day. The ability to identify the single most relevant point and make it memorable is useful whatever you do."

Deb Allen-Perry left the business in 1990, having worked at agencies including Charles Barker and Geers Gross.

She had wanted to be a copywriter from the age of 13, despite her headmistress describing it as "prostituting your talent for English."

Deb reckons advertising was easier in her era. "We had brave clients who wanted to push boundaries, we also had an audience who hadn't seen it all before and didn't have the attention span of guppies."

After leaving the creative department, she became a client ("how beastly I was to our agency creatives!"), working in internal communications.

She doesn't think she would want to come back to working in advertising. "I think advertising is a shadow of its former self," she remarks. "Press ads have become dull and illiterate. And there are still too many awards."

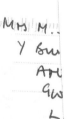

SHERBORNE

LA GRANDE ARCHE

MIAMI

INDONESIA

BERLIN

ACRONYMS

Here's a list of advertising's most common acronyms.

ACD

Associate creative director. Also known as creative group head. A creative who has responsibility for a group of accounts or creative teams.

AD

Art director. An ad agency creative who generally works with a copywriter; the two together forming a "creative team." Along with the copywriter, is responsible for coming up with the ideas for adverts. Has the additional responsibility of supervising the visual appearance of their executions.

AE

Account executive or, in some countries, "account handler." Person within an ad agency who acts as a liaison between the client and the rest of the agency, and has overall responsibility for the agency's business with that client.

CD

Creative director. Has overall responsibility for an agency's creative output on a specific account. Main duties include giving direction to the creative teams who are working on a brief.

CSD

Client services director. Person within an ad agency who is in overall charge of that agency's relationships with its clients.

CW

Copywriter. An ad agency creative who generally works with an art director, the two together forming a "creative team." Along with the art director, is responsible for coming up with the ideas for adverts. Has the additional responsibility of supervising any copy that is required.

DP

Director of photography. Supervises the lighting of a commercials shoot. May also operate the camera.

ECD

Executive creative director. In overall charge of the agency's entire creative output. Also responsible for the hiring and firing of creatives.

T&E

Travel and entertainment. Term for an amount of money allocated to an account or an individual for travel, taxis, lunches, and corporate entertainment. Not as much as it used to be.

Above-the-line: TV, print, and radio.

Account handler: person within an ad agency who acts as a liaison between the client and the rest of the agency, and has overall responsibility for the agency's business with that client.

Ambient: advertising that is found "out there in the environment" rather than in traditional media like newspapers and magazines. Examples include ads on the side of coffee cups, at the bottom of golf holes, and on sidewalks. The possibilities are endless.

Animatic: storyboards that have been filmed, with added sound effects and camera moves.

Art buyer: acts as a liaison between the agency and photographers and illustrators. Also advises creatives who to use.

Below-the-line: direct mail, and other "direct to consumer" advertising such as direct-response TV advertising as opposed to TV brand advertising.

Book: portfolio.

Brief: document written by the planner that explains what the client's requirements are for an advert, who the activity is being aimed at, what message they want to communicate, etc.

Campaign: a series of at least three advertisements on the same theme.

Creative director: has creative responsibility for one or more specific accounts, and is appointed by the agency's ECD (executive creative director), the person in overall charge of the department.

Digital advertising: activity that appears on the internet, such as banners, facebook apps, games, microsites, and virals.

Direct advertising: same as "below-the-line."

Engagement planner: if the account planner decides who the brand is going to talk to, the engagement planner decides what media should be used to reach them.

Grade: everything to do with the final look of a TV ad, for example how contrasty or color-saturated the film is. The process itself is known as grading.

Head of art: has overall responsibility for the imagery the agency sources for its print output. Advises creatives on which photographers and illustrators are right for a particular job.

Hotshop: small, highly creative agency.

Micro-network: an agency that aims to cover the world from a base of just one agency in each region, as opposed to one in each country.

Mood film: a film made of clips from movies or other ads, which demonstrates your idea.

Network agency: a group that has agencies in many countries. A network agency may have as many as 100 or 150 offices.

Offer ad: ad that offers the consumer a deal, e.g. BOGOF ("buy one get one free").

One-off ad: a single execution that is not part of a campaign.

Placement: time creatives spend working at an agency for little money, in the hope of getting hired. May be time-limited or open-ended. If things go well, a placement team gets "extended," i.e. asked to stay for longer.

Planner: person in an agency who is responsible for determining advertising strategy—who the brand will target, and what it will say to them.

Reference: images or film clips used to support/explain the idea for an ad.

Research: process in which an advertising idea is exposed to consumers. Their feedback may either kill the idea, green-light it, or suggest areas for "improvement."

Scam ads (sometimes known as chip shop ads or ghost ads): ads that teams create for the sole purpose of winning awards, rather than in response to a genuine client brief.

Scamp: a rough drawing used to get the idea for an ad across as simply as possible.

Script: description of what will happen in a TV or radio spot.

Shop: agency.

Spec ad/spec campaign: short for "speculative"—dummy ad/campaign that you've mocked up for your book rather than one that has actually run.

Storyboard: series of drawings that visualize the action of a TV or cinema ad.

Strategies: smart thinking about how to sell a product.

Tabletop ad: literally, an ad that is shot on a table. Often for food products.

Tactical ad: ads used "tactically" to capitalize on a specific event or occasion.

Through-the-line or integrated shop: agency that offers clients every service from TV advertising right through to point-of-sale materials.

Trade ad: ad featured in trade publications.

Traffic department: the team that manages the agency's workflow.

SUGGESTED READING

There are many, many books that aim to teach you how to create great advertising; far too many to list here.

If you are interested in reading more about the specific subject matter of this book—the skills needed to be successful as a creative above and beyond creating great ads—there are no books other than this one that deal exclusively with that subject, though there is quite a bit of relevant material in the excellent *Hey Whipple, Squeeze This*, by Luke Sullivan, specifically Chapter 8 (*The enemies of advertising*) and Chapter 9 (*Presenting and protecting your work*). However, most of the writing that goes beyond 'how to write adverts' is to be found on the internet.

I would humbly recommend my own blog *Scamp* (*scampblog.blogspot.com*), a dubiously useful advertising digest, but which does contain a collection of tips for young creatives.

Far better than my blog is that written by Dave Trott, co-founder of famous-in-the-80s British ad agency Gold Greenlees Trott, and currently running Chick Smith Trott. Dave Trott's blog (*cstadvertising.com/blog*) is a daily masterclass in the attitudes and behaviors that lead to success for creative people.

Someone called Alex Bogusky has also started a blog. Very, very interesting stuff. If you don't know it already, the web address is *http://alexbogusky.posterous.com/*.

I also recommend reading about how the world's top creatives approach the job, in their own words. There is an excellent series of creative profiles at *Creativity* magazine (*creativity-online.com*; the interviews are in their '*Creative Culture*' section), and at *ihaveanidea.org*.

In addition to acquainting yourself with the thoughts of the industry's leaders, I also think it's tremendously useful to know what's happening down in the trenches. There are several blogs written by young creative teams trying to break into the business, which are full of stories about how to approach placements, how to get in to see creative directors, and the like. The best known in the UK at the time of writing is *Creative in London* (*creativeinlondon.blogspot.com*) by Jai & Wal. However, by the time you read this, they will most likely have a job, and won't be blogging about how to get a job any more. But someone else will be.

ACKNOWLEDGEMENTS

Dedicated to Nick A.

Thanks to David Droga for the inspirational foreword.

Thanks to my interviewees—Trevor Beattie, Jeff Benjamin, Jeremy Craigen, Flo Heiss, Amir Kassaei, Siimon Reynolds, and Paul Silburn. And a thousand thanks too to Ruth Harlow, Antoinette de Lisser, Mindy Liu, Samantha Parfitt, Stephen Sapka, Meike Scharnhorst, and Tania Sukiennik for finding time in busy diaries.

Thanks to Deb Allen-Perry, Kevin Amter, Jamie Barrett, Paul Belford, James Best, Inky Blackstuff, Paul Burke, Neil Christie, James Cooper, Russell Davies, Mark Denton, Mark 'Copyranter' Duffy, Dave Dye, Elisa Edmonds, Alexandre Gama, Nick Gill, Bill Green, David Guerrero, David Hackworthy, Tim Harris, James Hayhurst, Sir John Hegarty, David Hieatt, Bob Hoffman, Richard Huntington, Fergus Hynd, John January, Davud Karbassioun, Ben Kay, Nick Kidney, Simon Learman, Owen Lee, Tanya Livesey, Lorelei Mathias, Jim Morris, Tom Morton, Grant Parker, Ewan Paterson, Ben Priest, Mark Reddy, Suzie Shaw, Francesco Taddeucci, Jo Tanner, Justin Tindall, Dave Trott, Nathalie Turton, Sarah Watson, Nikki Weinstein Maizel, and Simon Welsh, for all your help and advice, and apologies to anyone else I've forgotten.

Thanks to Ceri Amphlett for the wonderful illustrations.

Thanks to Chris Challinor, Matthew Croft, Oli Maltby, Rebecca Low, and everyone at The Chase for the fab design.

Thanks to everyone at Laurence King—Christina Borsi, Sophie Page, Gaynor Sermon, and especially Jo Lightfoot.

Thanks to June, Ruben, and Rachel for a lifetime of encouragement.

Love to Suzie, Sophie, and Coco.

PICTURE CREDITS

P16 Top: Chris Rush and Andy Peel, www.wearecrap.co.uk
Middle: Adam Chiappe & Saunby
Bottom right: Mike and Bern homepage
Copywriter: Bernard Hunter, Art Director: Mike Bond
Bottom left: Lucky dip. David Goss & Phoebe Coulton

P26 Budweiser labels. Copywriter & Art Director: Jeremy Craigen

P31 Top left: Modernista!
Top right: Wieden & Kennedy
Middle: Modernista!
Bottom left and right: Grey (London), BDGworkfutures

P32 Top: TBWA/Chiat Day (LA). Photography: Benny Chan
Middle: DDB Turkey
Bottom: Wieden & Kennedy

P35 Vodafone desk crusher. Creative direction: Flo Heiss/James Cooper, Art Direction: Dennis Christensen, Director: David McNulty, Flash: Adrian Rowbotham, Props Machine Shop

P44 Australian Youth Orchestra, Louis Armstrong. Siimon Reynolds

P49 VW Cops Polo. Photography: Paul Murphy, www.paulmurphy.com

P57 Labour Isn't Working, Conservative Party Archive Trust

P65 Courtesy of Crispin Porter + Bogusky

P85 Photography: Dan Tobin Smith

P98 The Grand Tour (for the National Gallery). Branding Agency: The Partners, Art Director: Jim Prior, Art Director: Greg Quinton, Design Director: Robert Ball, Project Manager: Donna Hemley, Project Manager: Andrew Webster, Designer: Kevin Lan, Designer: Paul Currah, Designer: Jay Lock, Copywriter: Jim Davies, Website: Digit London, Client: Danielle Chidlow, The National Gallery, Client: Dan Gates, Hewlett Packard, Photography: Brad Haynes (for Stubbs image), Mat Stuart, The Partners, Flickr

P112 Top: Matthieu Clainchard, Rassemblement Pour Repeindre (Gathering to Repaint) 2006
Bottom: Patrice Gaillard & Claude, Tokyo Grand Design, 2004, Hi-fi system, stereo amplifiers, loudspeakers, MDF, painting polyurethane, fabric, metal; 50 x 40 x 35 inches (each). Collection Domaine de Chamarande, France. Production 40m CUBE. Courtesy Galerie Loevenbruck, Paris

P117 Images © Paul Hartnett/PYMCA

P127 Labour Party: Be Afraid, Be Very Afraid. Trevor Beattie, (TWBA/London)

P128 Playstation: Mental Wealth; Fifi. Trevor Beattie, (TWBA/London)

P138 Portrait of Amir Kassaei. Photography: Oliver Helbig

P139 Portrait "Horst Schlämmer," DDB for Volkswagen

P139 Golf GTI—For boys who were always men, DDB for Volkswagen

P145 T-Mobile Dance—Life's for Sharing. Paul Silburn, Creative Partner, Saatchi & Saatchi London

P148 Mississippi Burning, Gene Hackman & William Dafoe, 1988. Director: Alan Parker. Orion/The Klobal Collection

P150 Miami image, © Roberto A Sanchez

Published in 2010 by
Laurence King Publishing Ltd
361–373 City Road
London EC1V 1LR
United Kingdom
Tel: +44 20 7841 6900
Fax: +44 20 7841 6910
e-mail: enquiries@laurenceking.com
www.laurenceking.com

A catalogue record for this book is available from the British Library.

ISBN: 978-1-85669-657-9

Design: The Chase www.thechase.co.uk
Typeface: PMN Caecilia
Illustrator: Ceri Amphlett www.ceriamphlett.co.uk
Photography (cover & dividers): Dave Sykes www.davidsykes.com
Senior Editors: Sophie Page and Gaynor Sermon

Printed in China.

LAURENCE KING